To E

A

believe

Love,
Roxie
Enget

THE REVEALED

Unraveling the Secrets of the Bible
You Won't Hear Sunday Morning

R. R. ENGET

WESTBOW
PRESS®
A DIVISION OF THOMAS NELSON
& ZONDERVAN

WestBow Press books may be ordered through booksellers or by contacting:

WestBow Press
A Division of Thomas Nelson & Zondervan
1663 Liberty Drive
Bloomington, IN 47403
www.westbowpress.com
844-714-3454

All Scripture quotations are taken from the New King James Version®. Copyright © 1982 by Thomas Nelson. Used by permission. All rights reserved.

ISBN: 978-1-6642-4806-9 (sc)
ISBN: 978-1-6642-4807-6 (hc)
ISBN: 978-1-6642-4805-2 (e)

Library of Congress Control Number: 2021921664

Print information available on the last page.

WestBow Press rev. date: 6/25/2022

TABLE OF CONTENTS

INTRODUCTION

This Bible study has been an exciting adventure. The words seemed to fly onto each page as I held my MacBook, sitting cross-legged on my bed during the Covid-19 Pandemic. My goal was to lay out the Bible in an organized way that helps make the Bible more understandable.

The Bible can be confusing if you don't pull away and see it with a telescopic perspective. Oftentimes, we look at a passage and don't think of how it fits in the whole narrative of the Bible. That's what I hope to do with this overall method of addressing the Bible.

Think of understanding the Bible as comparing it to a body. The body needs the skeleton to give form, and the flesh covers your skeleton and completes the body. This Bible study is the skeleton only. The flesh or the details can be added later.

I looked at scripture the wrong way when I was young. I opened the Bible to a page and put my finger on a verse with my eyes closed. I opened my eyes, read that verse, and thought God was speaking to me through that random verse. That memory makes me chuckle, now. I know that wasn't the way God intended His Word to be read.

Before we begin this study, I want to clarify how to study the Bible. It is threefold:

o   contextually
o   grammatically
o   historically

First, read it in *context*. Grabbing an isolated verse without context can make it say something it doesn't. Read all the scriptures around it, think of who wrote it, and ask some questions such as the following:

o Was it before or after the death and resurrection of Jesus?
o Is it part of the Gospel of Grace?
o To whom was this passage or book meant for? Jews or Gentiles?
o Was it written while the Jews were under the law?

Secondly, as you read the Bible, note the *grammar.* Watch for verb and subject changes and the different words used for God.

Lastly, know the *history* surrounding the passage. What were the politics and customs of that time?

Since very few of us can read Hebrew or Greek, we rely on the translators. Listed are some of the ways the translators agreed to treat the scriptures.

1. How they translated the names of God are important to define. For example:

   • The name of *Elohim* was translated as *God.* It is a plural noun and suggests the mystery of the Trinity (Genesis 1).
   • *El* is translated as *God* in singular—for example, El Shaddai (God Almighty) as used in Genesis 17:1, and El Roi (God Who Sees) as used in Genesis 16:13.
   • *YHWH/*Yahweh/Jehovah was translated as LORD (all capitals). It's God's holy covenant name, used primarily for God's covenant people in the Old Testament (Jews). Yahweh/YHWH/Jehovah's definition is "to be." In Exodus 3:14, "God said to Moses, I AM Who I AM," which means the Self-Existent One, always was and always will be.
   • *Adonai* is translated as "Lord" (lowercase letters). It is a substitution for Yahweh/YHWH/Jehovah, out of reverence for God's covenant name. Moses's dialogue

with God in Exodus 4:10–12, is a good example. "Then Moses said to the LORD, O my Lord ..." Moses would not say God's holy name out loud, so he used Adonai for the second Lord. Many Jewish people today will not utter the name of God or write it out fully because of their respect for the majesty and holiness of God (e.g., Yahweh is YHWH; God is G _d in written form).

- El Elyon is "God Most High" (Genesis 14:18). It was used for the Gentiles, who were not under the covenants with the LORD/Yahweh/YHWH, but were included after Christ's resurrection.

2. The translators will add words to the translation that you will not find in the original. Those are in *italics*. Italicized words are used to smooth out the translation. I oftentimes read the passage without the added words just to check if the meaning stays the same.

Is the Bible the True Word of God?

"Why do you believe the Word of God is true?" I remember being asked that question on a chilly fall day in 1982, while eating lunch with a friend at the University of North Dakota. I was tongue-tied and ill equipped to fully answer that question. That incident caused me to think my answer through, and later I became prepared to answer that question. Here is my answer today.

I believe God's Word is true because:

1. It is an intricate book of sixty-six individual books, written by forty authors over 1,600 years, and yet it agrees and fits together as one book. Every word of the scriptures is God-breathed, and He used spirit-filled Jewish men to write those books (Romans 3:1-2).

2. The Bible has 1,239 prophecies in the Old Testament and 578 in the New Testament, for a total of 1,817 according to J. Barton Payne's *Encyclopedia of Biblical Prophecy*. Many prophecies are fulfilled, and others are waiting to be fulfilled as God carries out His plan. A good description of fulfilled prophecies is the book *Fulfilled Prophecies and Other Evidence That the Bible Is the Word of God* by Matthew McGee. There is no other book that fulfills its prophesies to the letter as the Bible does.

3. The Jewish people's existence. The Jews' supernatural two-thousand-year survival outside of their land (after 70 A.D.) and their miraculous return to the Promised Land (Israel) in 1948 is simply amazing. One good resource is *Supernatural or Just Remarkable?* which was written by Ariel Hyde from *Jewish Voice*.

4. My personal faith and testimony. Jesus lives inside of me, and He lives in every believer who has come to a saving knowledge of Him. Jesus is real.

How Does This Class Function?

In the first class, we will go over the main introduction and the first week's introduction. At home, you are encouraged to complete the following "five days" on your own.

When you arrive the following week, we will review and discuss the five days you completed that week. We will continue with that pattern until final eighth week.

There are many scriptures to look up each day. This study uses the New King James Version. I encourage you to look up all the scriptures and make notes in your Bible or a designated notebook. I encourage you to find and use a *Strong's Concordance*. *Strong's* will help you find the exact meaning of a Hebrew or Greek word, and you don't need to speak or read the language.

I also included scriptures that we fly through as we cover the

Bible in seven lessons. I would love for you to read all the scriptures but that may not be possible! Do your best, but also use it as a guide for what part of the Bible we are studying for each lesson.

Show, Don't Tell

Finally, I want emphasize that I want to *show* you what I have found and not *tell* you what you should think. It's important that we search out the scriptures for ourselves and allow the Holy Spirit to lead each of us. It said in 1 Corinthians 2:10, "But God has revealed them to us through His Spirit. For the Spirit searches all things, yes, the deep things of God." God encourages us to search and understand the scriptures. We need to equip ourselves to defend our faith. Here is a scripture I would like to leave with you. Don't forget to pray and ask God to help and guide you before each study.

> "Be diligent to present yourself approved to God, a worker who does not need to be ashamed, rightly dividing the word of truth." (2 Timothy 2:15)

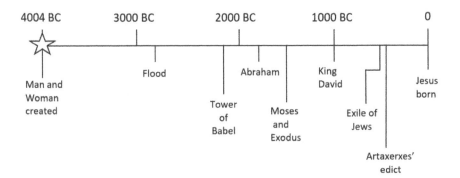

4004 BC	3000 BC	2000 BC	1000 BC	0

Man and Woman created

Flood

Tower of Babel

Abraham

Moses and Exodus

King David

Exile of Jews

Artaxerxes' edict

Jesus born

Lesson 1

GENESIS AND MARRIAGE

"And in the beginning God created the heavens and the earth."
—Genesis 1:1

I grew up in a small North Dakota town and completed my high school years in a class of fifty-two students. I had known every one of my classmates since kindergarten and most of my teachers for many years. But I started feeling uncomfortable in some of my classes because my science teachers began laughing about foolish people who believed in the creation story from the Bible. I wondered, too, at times, if we believed in some "big Genesis fairy tale." Evolution seemed so rational in the 1970s as I was being introduced to it.

I remember one bright spring morning when one of my science teachers gleefully crowed in class that scientists would soon know how life began. He victoriously claimed the "simple cell" was soon to be unlocked from all its secrets and we would know how the universe began. He said our scientists would soon prove that life could be created by some simple chemical reactions and a Superior Being/God wasn't necessary. As my teacher spoke, I stood up from my desk, in a flash, and I told my teacher he was wrong!

OK, that didn't happen. I actually slid lower in my desk and didn't lock eyes with my teacher that day or many days after that. I wasn't equipped to deal with defending my faith at age sixteen. I wasn't prepared. I am now equipped to answer and the following *"For Further Study"* would have been valuable at that time.

For further study: *The Case for the Creator by Lee Strobel.*

This book lays out the basics that support a Creator-God. Lee Strobel's book demonstrates how only an intelligent-designer could have created this complex universe. The following four points stand in the way of any other explanation for how the universe came into existence.

1. *Everything cannot come from nothing.*
2. *Chaos will not turn into ordered information.*
3. *Non-life cannot transition into a living being.*
4. *Unconsciousness cannot transform into consciousness.*

Flash forward a few years later. I entered a Christian university at my dad's request. *Finally!* I thought when I arrived at my first day of college. *I will be one of the best-equipped students here.*

Since birth, I had attended Sunday school every Sunday and countless summer vacation Bible schools at various churches. In my teen years, I had taught Sunday school and VBS to younger children, retelling the stories I had learned. I participated in Bible studies and went faithfully to church camp every year. With all that preparation, I undoubtedly would excel at a Christian university!

What I didn't realize was that Bible stories were important, but they didn't tell the Bible's complete message that God has revealed to us. I actually knew very little.

At my Christian university, one of my college professors repeatedly said that if you understood the book of Genesis, you were nearly halfway to understanding the Bible as a whole. That was great news for me, but I still lacked the knowledge to put all the pieces together. My knowledge of the Bible stories wasn't enough. I needed more.

That same professor also said that the book of Genesis began the framework for all the next sixty-five books of the Bible. Genesis set the stage. The remaining sixty-five books refer to the book of Genesis over and over. Genesis covered Adam and Eve's sin (fall) to Joseph's time in Egypt. Genesis' fifty chapters are a very significant two thousand years after Adam and Eve sinned. I gained a lot of knowledge at my Christian university, but I didn't come away understanding how it fit together. The message was still unclear. It seemed complex and hard to understand. I floundered at times.

Since then, I have learned a lot, and I would like to show the form of this wonderful book we call the Bible. It tells the greatest story ever told! I won't retell those wonderful stories of the characters of the Bible but just concentrate on the basics. Filling in the rest of the richness of the scriptures would take more than a lifetime of study. (I know it is one of the most exciting endeavors you will ever take on.)

I have included a time line at the top of most lesson pages. The time line begins at Adam's creation and ends at the birth of Christ. The time line will help to distinguish how quickly the Bible moved through some parts of human history and how the narrative of the Bible slowed on the time line when the call of Abraham begins. The history of the Jews compiles most of the Old Testament, with the exception of the first eleven chapters of Genesis.

DAY 1

CREATION WAS NOT SIMPLE

In Sunday school, when I was a child, a creation lesson was simply taught. The six creation days were briefly spoken of, and then we went on to the "day of rest" on day seven. Our lesson took up one Sunday morning in our Sunday school curriculum. It was more of a lesson on resting than the creation story. It didn't help equip me for those evolutionary science classes I later encountered. So let's go a little deeper.

First of all, who wrote Genesis? *Moses did.*

Moses was a Hebrew/Jew, and an adopted Egyptian prince. He was educated in the Egyptian Palace around 1500 B.C. Jesus said that Moses (who wrote the first five books of the Bible) wrote of Him (Jesus) in John 5:46. Moses was inspired by God as all the authors of the Bible were.

Read Genesis 1–2:1

How is a day structured in the creation account given in Genesis? Take a look at Genesis 1:5, 8, 13, 19, 23, and 31.

God structured the day to begin in the evening and the Jews still follow that pattern. The evening begins a new day. The new day would begin at 6:00 p.m. in the evening and end the next day at 6:00 p.m. Very different from our midnight-to-midnight days we are accustomed to in modern times. This is important to keep in mind throughout the scriptures.

My husband and I visited Israel in 2014. There, it was very evident that the Sabbath (Shabbat/Saturday) began on Friday evening at six. Our Jewish guide was very anxious to leave us at noon on Friday so she could cook before the Sabbath (Saturday) that would begin in six hours. (No work on the Sabbath was allowed, including meal preparation.) Our guide left us to figure out what to do with the rest of the afternoon on Friday. Everything was going to come to a crawl on Friday evening from six until Saturday at six in the evening. There wasn't much to do. We didn't see our guide again until Sunday morning.

Notice how the first two verses of Genesis 1 are not part of the six-creation day narrative. The creation of the earth wasn't included in the creation story. Could the earth already been in existence? Read the following "For Further Study" and give us your insight.

For Further Study:
Read Ezekiel 28:11–17 and Jude 6. After reading these passages, think about the following questions. When could this event with Lucifer have happened? _____. Where did this take place? _____

Why didn't God say in Genesis 1:1, "God created everything or the universe"? Instead, God separated it into two parts, (1) the heavens, and (2) the earth. In the last book of the Bible in Revelation 21:1, it told us, the curse would be lifted in the future. It said "And I saw a new heaven and a new earth." The heavens and the earth will be still separated in two parts even after they will be made anew after the Millennium ends. God had a reason for that.

Consider the "heaven and earth" as a promise divider.

The earth refers to the promises given to the Jews—they are all earthly promises. The Jews look for an earthly King and an earthly kingdom. The scriptures told them, the "Kingdom of Heaven" would be here on earth (Micah 4:1-4; Daniel 7:27).

The heavens are promises for the bride of Christ or the church.

Ephesians 1:3 and Philippians 3:20 told us (the body of Christ) that our spiritual blessings are in the "heavenly places" and our "citizenship is in heaven."

Let's take an in-depth look at the creation verses and verbs used to describe creation. Fill out the following table:

What appeared or was created in first chapter of Genesis each day?	What verb/verb phrase did God use on each day?
Day 1 (vs. 3–5)	
Day 2 (vs. 6–8)	
Day 3 (vs. 9–13)	
Day 4 (vs. 14–19)	
Day 5 (vs. 20–23)	
Day 6 (vs. 24–31)	

Questions to ponder:

Notice the verbs used on each creation day; they vary. Why does God use various verbs for on the days of creation? _____

Does it appear to you that possibly some parts of the creation had already been created? _____

DAY 2

THE PLURALITY OF GOD (TRINITY)

Genesis 1:26: "Then God said, 'Let _____ make man in _____ image, according to _____ likeness.'"

The Trinity was a concept clearly referenced in the New Testament. What did the Jews know about the plurality of God before the New Testament was written and before Christ's first advent? Jews who don't accept Jesus as their Messiah still struggle with the idea that "God is one and yet three Persons" today.

What compounds their confusion is the Shema, a prayer that many Jews still say two times a day. Found in Deuteronomy 6:4, it begins like this: "Hear, O Israel: the LORD our God, the LORD is one." They stumble over the Trinity concept when they read the LORD is one.

Look up the following scriptures. Was there enough revelation given from God in the Old Testament for the Jews to know that God was/is multiple in Persons and yet one God? Was The Trinity referred to in any Old Testament references? Read the references below. (They didn't have the advantage of the New Testament since it was written after Jesus' resurrection.)

Genesis 3:22 _____

Genesis 11:7 _____

Psalm 2:3-7 _____

Psalm 110:1 _____

Isaiah 6:8 _____

For Further Study:

Nabeel Qureshi wrote "Seeking Allah Finding Jesus". The Trinity is wonderfully explained in his book. Nabeel, as a former Muslim, also struggled with the concept of the Trinity, in the same way the Jews would struggle with it.

Let's continue on with Genesis 1:26. It said, "Make man in Our Image." What comprises the image of God? _____
God is spirit (John 4:24–26). The image of God is not a physical body form. But rather "the image of God" is comprised of mind, emotions, and will. Would you agree? _____
I love the New Testament story which illustrated this concept in Mark 12:13-18. The Pharisees brought Jesus a silver coin, trying to trick Him. They asked Him, "Is it lawful to pay taxes to Caesar?"
Jesus took the coin and asked the Pharisees, "Whose image and inscription is this?
They answered, "Caesar's."
And Jesus said, "Render to Caesar the things that are Caesar's and to God the things that are God's."
What Jesus didn't go on to say was, humankind is stamped with God's image (*mind* and *emotions*) just as the coin was stamped with Caesars' image. I think the Pharisees understood what Jesus was saying, and let it drop. They knew we are made in God's image and can choose (the *will*) to belong to Him. The coin can go to Caesar.
The following illustration is a visual of how we are made in God's image. Our body surrounds our soul and spirit. Our body helps us interpret what is around us through our five senses. The soul contains the mind, emotions, and will. The spirit connects us to God if we believe and take God at His word. This diagram illustrates Adam and Eve's condition before they sinned.

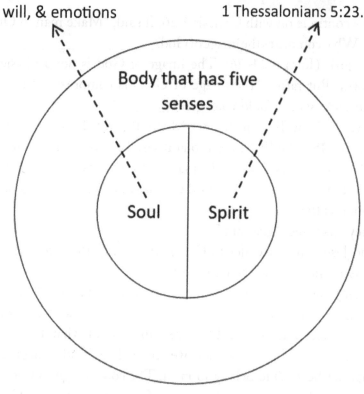

Soul has mind, will, & emotions

Adam and Eve's spirits were connected to God's spirit, Hebrews 4:12 and 1 Thessalonians 5:23.

Body that has five senses

Soul

Spirit

DAY 3

WHERE WAS EVE?

Read Genesis 2.

In Genesis 2:4 the name for God (Elohim) changed to _____ God (Jehovah Elohim). The change indicated which One of the Godhead stepped out to create the heavens and the earth. As often happens in the scriptures, the Old Testament revealed truths and the New Testament explained them in more detail.

Look up the scriptures in the New Testament that revealed our Creator.

Colossians 1: 13-16
Ephesians 3:9
John 1:3, 10
Hebrews 1:2
1 Corinthians 8:6

Who is our Creator? _____

Think of this: Four thousand years after creation, Jesus, our Creator, hung on the cross, a tree He had created became the means to murder Him. The soldiers hurt and mocked their Creator. Jesus knew every detail about of those soldiers and had them in mind before time began. He hung on the cross, succumbing to it as a Lamb to slaughter as the creation unknowingly crucified their Creator.

Christ humbled Himself to the point of death because He loves every one of us and became sin for us.

Let's continue on with the creation story concerning the woman. (Adam named his wife Eve after they disobeyed God in the next chapter of Genesis. God referred to her as the "woman.") Was the woman created on the sixth day at the same time as Adam? _____

This is a complex but important question. It affects how we perceive our relationship with our spouses and our relationship with Christ as His bride. Was the woman an afterthought? Or was she possibly created last as the ultimate creation, God's finest achievement? I've heard it both ways. Scripture supports neither explanation.

Genesis 1:27: When was the woman created? _____

Genesis 5:1-2: Were the man and woman created on the same day? _____How is it possible they were created on the same day if the woman wasn't there with Adam on the day of his creation? _____

Contrast the verbs used in Genesis 2:8 for the man's creation _____ and Genesis 2:22 for the woman's. _____. God used a different verb regarding each one, because it was a different process for each time. The word for Adam's creation was "formed" because it was like a potter with clay forming Adam. The verb for the woman was "made" because she was assembled from the man.

Let's look at the following verse a little more closely. Genesis 2:24 said, "Therefore a man shall leave his father and his mother and be joined to his wife: and they shall become _____."

Notice in the first part of the verse, the woman was not told to leave her father and mother; only the man was told to leave his father and mother. I always felt that it was for the woman's protection, especially if the husband was gone for various reasons (e.g., wars, farming large pieces of land, livestock care).

We lived in Islamabad, Pakistan, in the mid-1980s. We had a cook who lived with us. He had a wife and children who lived several hours away, in a little village. Zeman traveled four hours by bus to see his family every two weeks. After noticing the lost time with his family, I suggested that he bring his family to stay at our home so he could see them every evening. Zeman told me he wouldn't consider it because his wife would have to leave her family if she came to live with us. He felt she was safer with her parents.

I think that is still the mentality in some areas overseas. Family provides the protection because protection from police or government is broken or nonexistent. Also, staying at home, near parents, when children are young, has its advantages. Finding a reliable babysitter is a worldwide problem.

Let's continue with the latter part of the Genesis 2:24, "they shall become one flesh." "Ehad" is the Hebrew word for "one." It means "a composite." I love this part. The man and woman were literally together in one body immediately after creation. After Adam named the animals, he noted that all the animals had a complement or other half. God waited for Adam to desire a mate. When Adam did, the LORD God placed Adam into a deep sleep. He took one of Adam's sides (see "For Further Study" for why I am not using the word "rib") to assemble the woman. Immediately after Adam awoke, the man and woman became one flesh again, through marriage. The woman was present from the moment of humankind's (Adam's) creation. She was him and was part of him and waiting for God to assemble her from Adam's side. It also depicted how God looks at marriage.

For Further Study:

The word for "rib" in the scriptures was translated from the Hebrew word "tsela". Tsela was translated 40 times as "side" throughout scripture. This is the only occurance when it was translated as "rib" and is a poor translation. Please read an article written by Wayne Simpson, <u>Adam's Rib</u>, on jasher. com that gives more information. Does it make sense that the woman was taken out of man's side(not rib) and Eve was Adam's literal other half rather than a single rib bone? _____ " Side" also helps explain why

Adam decribed the woman as "bone of my bone and flesh of my flesh." "Flesh of my flesh" wouldn't make sense with a solitary rib bone.

While the man and woman both have their unique personalities and roles, they still are one in flesh. It is the only relationship that makes a good comparison to the Trinity. The Godhead is one Being (Composite), but God the Father, God the Son, and God the Holy Spirit each have different personalities and roles. They are different but equal, one combined Being but three personalities/roles.

The marriage theme runs throughout the scriptures. Two thousand years later, after the creation of man and woman, the LORD (Jehovah) became a "husband" (Jeremiah 31:32; Isaiah 54:5) to the Jewish nation. God became one with His people.

The same concept is used in the New Testament with the church being the Bride of Christ and Christ is the Bridegroom. At salvation, we are joined to Christ's body just as the woman and the man were "one flesh" at the beginning of creation. How does this apply to our relationship with Jesus? Read Ephesians 5:30-32 (NKJV). We are _____ of His body, of His flesh and His bones. Read Romans 8:17b: "we may be _____together." Second Timothy 2:12a said, "We shall also _____ with Him." What did Jesus say about a husband and wife in Mark 10:8-9? Are they one or two flesh? _____

We are literally Christ's flesh after we accept Christ's marriage proposal by putting our faith and trust in Jesus. According to Jewish custom, the bridegroom paid a bride price called a "mohar". After payment, the bridegroom then left for home, to prepare a place for his willing, betrothed bride. The bridegroom's father would let his son know when he could return for his bride. The father decided when the home, his son prepared, was complete. After the father deemed all was ready, he would tell his son to go get his bride and only then was son free to do that.

The bride's duty was to be ready for her bridegroom to return at any moment. Can you think of the time, Christ, our Bridegroom, paid a price for his Bride the church? _____Where is our

Bridegroom now? _____ (John 14:2-3) In Matthew 24:36 Jesus said "But of that day and hour no one knows, not even the angels of heaven but _____." Jesus as the Son of God has voluntarily restricted His knowledge of Own return because He is waiting for His Father's approval before He returns for His Bride.

DAY 4

THE BIG LIE

Read Genesis 3

I don't know about you, but I don't like snakes. I wasn't always that way. When I was young, I used to chase my boy cousins with a live snake in my hand. I often kept pet snakes hidden in our home's back entry in a coffee can with holes punched in the plastic lid. My mom would find my coffee can, and she immediately knew who had placed it there, and what creature was inside. I would hear my name being called. By my mother's tone of voice, I knew that I was in trouble. She had found it. My mother was not in favor of my choice of pets. Those days are long past. Now snakes make me shudder.

Satan used a snake to speak to the woman. It must have been a different-looking reptile at that point because the woman wasn't repulsed. She wasn't surprised by the snake's ability to speak either. Before the woman had been taken out of Adam, the LORD instructed Adam not to eat from the tree of _____ (Genesis 2:16–17). The woman added to the original command that Adam was given. She said to the serpent, "Nor shall you _____ it" (Genesis 3:3). Since that wasn't part of the original command, does that sound like she had second-hand information to you? Perhaps after having relayed the instructions to his wife, could Adam have added for more emphasis, saying, "Don't even touch it"? What do you think? _____

Let's look at the sequence of events.

- The serpent questioned the woman (Genesis 3:1).
- The woman responded (Genesis 3:2-3).
- The serpent and the *big lie* (Genesis 3:4—"You will ____ surely die").
- The woman _____ (Genesis 3:6)
- Where was Adam's location? (Genesis 3:6) _____
- She gave it to Adam, and he _____ (Genesis 3:6).
- *Then* their eyes were opened (Genesis 3:7—notice, both of them had to disobey before their eyes were opened; they were one flesh).

Did they die? _____

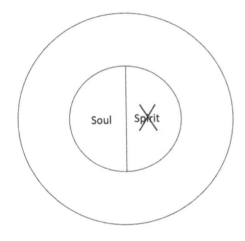

Spiritual connection to God died after the woman and the man disobeyed God

At that moment, when they had both eaten the fruit, the woman and the man died (separated from God) spiritually. We often think of death as the cessation of bodily functions, and our bodies lose our spirits at the loss of those functions. But God sees death as "separation from Him." Adam and Eve were now separated from God spiritually. They were dead.

Their bodies had begun to die as well. That would take longer. Their connection to God was severed, *but* when they admitted guilt, they were reconnected spiritually to the Spirit of God. But the curse was now in effect. Their bodies had begun to die, but their spirits would live eternally with God.

Read the following verses. 1 Corinthians 15:21-22: "For as in Adam _____, even so in Christ all shall be made alive." Ephesians 2:1: "And you He _____, who were dead in trespasses and sins."

Think About It: *Everyone born after the fall of Adam and Eve, is born spiritually dead. Our spirits at physical birth aren't connected to God. To connect our spirits to God, we need to choose to put our faith in Jesus and then we are born in the Spirit. Jesus said, "_____, he cannot see the kingdom of God." John 3:3b. Mankind's sin brought death-separation from God into the world. That was never God's intent. He created us for life, life eternally with Him. We must be born again.*

My husband worked for a company for more than thirty years. The company's spouses associaton provided many activities and special interest groups for spouses' participation. I really enjoyed this benefit. I was involved in many of the activities provided by that association, such as French class, coffee groups, and bird watching. Most of my friends were part of the group too.

But when my husband unexpectedly retired, my participation was over too. I was informed that I was no longer welcome at those activities because we were no longer part of the company. I was cut off. I was devastated. When Adam and Eve ate that fruit, they suddenly were disconnected from God. It was sudden, and until they were reconnected, they were dead and cut off from God.

Genesis 3:7b: "And they knew that they _____." What had changed? What made them aware that they were naked since before they hadn't realized it? Has that puzzled you? It puzzled me for years. Read the following scriptures to see what loss/change had come about: Job 29:14; Isaiah 64:6, 61:10; Psalm 132:16.

Who sinned? Was it Adam, Eve or both of them? _____

Read these scriptures for the answer.

1 Timothy 2:14
Romans 5:12-17

We really don't know what the woman was thinking. The various translations of the scriptures said she was "beguiled," "deceived," or "tricked." But Adam went forward with a clear head. I've heard many explanations for his willful sinfulness. Some theologians assert he wanted to join his beautiful wife, because he would have been separated from her forever if he hadn't sinned. My take is that he simply wanted to be "like God." What are your thoughts?

DAY 5

THE BLAME GAME

We lived in Anaco, Venezuela, from 1989 to 1991 in a three-bedroom concrete home that had been constructed in the 1950s. An attachment to the house served as a laundry room and an external bathroom. Petra, the woman we employed to assist with household work, spent time there washing and folding clothes. While working one day, she saw a snake popping its head in and out of the toilet bowl, apparently looking for an exit. The snake kept disappearing and resurfacing. She ran into the house to tell me. That's when the panic ensued.

When the house was built, the builders never put sewer traps on the pipes leading to the toilets. So the toilets were wide open to whatever vermin decided to come to the surface. Petra also told the gardener about the snake, which she had decided was poisonous. Our faithful gardener, armed with a garden spade, came to help. More people gathered excitedly, waiting for that unfortunate snake to show his head again. Within the hour, the panicked snake came shooting out of the stool, trying to make his getaway. The unfazed gardener was waiting with his spade and "bruised the snake's head." That is the picture I envision that day in the future, when Satan will be defeated once and for all.

After sinning, Adam and his wife each blamed someone other than themselves after eating the fruit. But when both of them did admit guilt, they were restored to fellowship with the LORD (their spirits were reconnected). But the world had changed in that moment when they disobeyed. Their bodies began to die, and creation began to suffer. Death entered the world.

God gave them hope for the future. The hope is in Genesis 3:15 NKJV: God spoke to the serpent, "And I will put _____ between you and the woman, and between your seed and her Seed; He shall bruise your head and you shall bruise His heel."

Who was "her Seed" (Galatians 3:16)? _____
Whose heel was bruised (Isaiah 53:5)? _____
Who will be crushed or have the head bruised (Romans 16:20)?

> Romans 8:19-22 NKJV summarized how everything changed in the moment of Adam's disobedience. "For the earnest expectation of the creation eagerly waits for the revealing of the sons of God. For the creation _____, but because of Him who subjected it in hope; because the creation itself also _____ into the glorious liberty of the children of God. For we know that the whole creation _____ and labors with the birth pangs together until now."

Adam and Eve suffered spiritual death (which was reconnected, when they admitted guilt) and they began to die physically.

After reading the above passage, what is our hope for the future? _____ As it said above in Romans 8, the creation groans. Take a look at the second law of thermodynamics in the box below that gives an explanation of how the "groaning" takes place.

Two Laws of Thermodynamics

*The **first law** is-Energy can neither be created nor destroyed. It can only change form. The first law agrees with the following scripture:*

Genesis 2:1, "Thus the heavens and the earth, and all the host of them, _____." God declared creation finished, nothing more was created, a closed system.

*The **second law** is- the entropy (gradual decline into disorder) of any isolated system always increases. Isaiah 24:6 stated, "Therefore the _____ has devoured the earth". The second law is in effect today.* Romans 5:19 says, "For as by one man's disobedience many were made sinners, so also by one Man's obedience many will be made righteous."

Who made us sinners? _____ Who can make us righteous?

_____

God has a plan of redemption that He revealed in His Word. Our next lesson will illustrate how sin overtook the earth and God's continuing mercy.

Lesson 1 Review

When was the woman created? _____
What was the "big lie" told by the serpent? _____
Did Adam and the woman die when they ate the fruit?

_____

Notes

Notes

Lesson 2

SO MUCH FAILURE!

Genesis' first eleven chapters took place over two thousand years. That's a lot of history in a few short chapters. And it's not very pretty. In this lesson, we will cover the period from Adam's sin until Abraham's call from God. The increasing effects of sin became more and more evident and were unstoppable.

Have you ever tried to stop the unstoppable? I experienced Hurricane Harvey in Houston in 2017. In the eight years we had lived in Houston, we had often experienced heavy rainfalls. I had also previously lived five years in tropical Venezuela. I thought I knew what a deluge looked like.

During the monsoon season in Venezuela, I would always try to get home before 4:00 p.m. because the afternoon rains would begin around that time. You could be stranded for an hour or two, wherever you were. If I were caught on the road, I would join the traffic that pulled over to the side of the road and waited. Rain came down in sheets. Windshield wipers could not keep up with the downpour. Then, at about 5:00 p.m., the rains would suddenly stop. Traffic would start moving again, and we would go our way.

Hurricane Harvey was the same but also different. Similarly, bucket-like water fell from the sky, but the difference was it didn't stop after an hour. We lived in a cul-de-sac. During the long five hours of heavy rainfall, all my neighbors and I emerged at the same time to helplessly observe our dilemma. The rain was intense and unusual, even for Houstonians. It might have been fascinating if we hadn't been so concerned about flooding. The street drainage system couldn't keep up. The drain overflow was rapidly creeping up our sidewalks threatening to enter our homes. It was a matter of time. The hurricane cell hung over our part of the city, pulling water from the gulf, never letting up for a minute. It was unstoppable.

The spread of sin over that newly created world was similar. Just like that water rapidly creeping up our sidewalks, sin was just as unstoppable. Rebellion increased, and God was forgotten. Let's take a look at these failures.

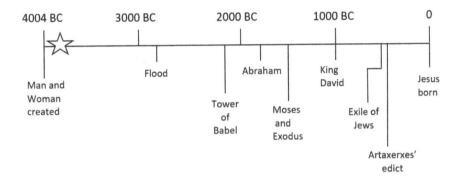

| 4004 BC | 3000 BC | 2000 BC | 1000 BC | 0 |

Man and Woman created

Flood

Tower of Babel

Abraham

Moses and Exodus

King David

Exile of Jews

Artaxerxes' edict

Jesus born

DAY 1

MURDER

Read Genesis 4

Have you had one of those fights with your siblings that caused a rage to explode inside of you? When growing up, my mom enrolled my two sisters and me in our church choir. Our practice time was every Sunday evening after evening church. At one particular practice, my sisters and I were all impatient. It was the end of the semester, and we all needed to get home and study for exams. Of course, the fact that we hadn't started studying earlier was no one's fault but our own.

I was already tense when our choir director decided to keep us later to perfect a new song. I thought, *let me out of here!* My middle sister had been teasing me all during practice. She laughingly whispered that I should have studied earlier and I wouldn't have this problem. I leaned over and grabbed the skin on her arm and twisted it—hard! She was a tough tomboy type of girl, but when I saw her eyes tear up, I knew I had gone too far.

My pride made me pretend I didn't care! My other sister turned to me and said in a stage whisper, "You are so mean!" She was right, but in my mind, I had every excuse in the book to defend my actions. My sister had made me mad. I blamed my actions on her.

Cain was more than just annoyed. He actually wanted to kill his younger brother. I would guess Abel had been angering Cain for a while.

Take a look at Genesis 4:3, where it says, "And in the process of time." This tells you that the two brothers had been instructed on how to make a sacrifice and how to do it in the manner that God desired. It wasn't the first time they had made a sacrifice. Cain's sacrifice didn't measure up. Cain knew what God wanted. He chose to do it his own way.

And then the LORD said to Cain in Genesis 4:6, "Why are you angry? And why has _____? If you do well, will you not be accepted? And if you do not do well _____. And its desire is for you but you should rule over it."

The LORD was interested in what Cain was feeling, and the LORD was giving him every chance to change his heart. Notice God was speaking directly to Cain. Then the LORD told him "sin lies at the door." The word for "sin" in Hebrew can also indicate, "sin offering." (Use Strong's Concordance) Sin offering is a literal animal such as a sheep that had four legs (quadruped). The LORD had left an animal for sacrifice at the door of Cain's dwelling, and Cain could go grab it. He wouldn't need to ask his sheepherder brother, Abel, for an animal to sacrifice. We don't know if Cain did this, but we do know that Cain's heart didn't change.

Read verse 8: "And Cain talked with Abel his brother: and it came to pass ..." And it came to pass. Does that lead you to believe that Cain had had a plan to get rid of his brother for a while? _____ We call that premeditated murder.

Read verses 13-15. After killing his brother, did Cain show any remorse? _____ What was he concerned about? _____

The LORD protected Cain from harm. God gave him

a mark so others wouldn't slay him. Why was the LORD merciful? _____

Read verse 16. "And Cain went out from the presence of the LORD." Cain ran from the LORD and possibly from his own family. Why do you think he left? _____

There were other events that occurred in this chapter that reveal the decline of humankind. Polygamy began in Genesis 4:19. The LORD was very careful to show in the creation of man how Adam/humankind was one woman and one man and they became one flesh through marriage. That was being destroyed by polygamy. There were also threats of killing/murder in Genesis 4:23–24. Man had turned away from the LORD.

Failure once again, but yet there was hope.

I can imagine that Eve felt so much joy and hope when Cain was born. She knew the LORD had a plan to redeem them. In Genesis 4:1, Eve said, "I have acquired a man from the LORD." She may have thought Cain was the Messiah, the one sent to redeem them. If she did, when she learned of his sin, she knew Cain was not the redeemer. Sin's effects had made itself known. Abel, her son, who was the man of _____, was dead (Hebrews 11:4). Her other son, Cain, was on the lam. They had a broken family. Adam and Eve conceived again and had another son, named Seth. He was born when Adam was (Genesis 5:3) _____ years old. "Then men began _____ on the name of the LORD" (Genesis 4:26b). Seth began a new godly line.

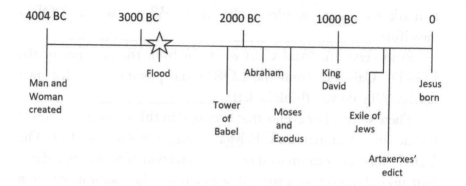

4004 BC   3000 BC   2000 BC   1000 BC   0

Flood

Abraham

King David

Jesus born

Man and Woman created

Tower of Babel

Moses and Exodus

Exile of Jews

Artaxerxes' edict

DAY 2

NOAH, THE ONLY RIGHTEOUS PERSON

Read Genesis 5 and 6

I didn't want to move to China in 2001. We were living in Oklahoma, and I told my husband that I didn't want to go overseas again. We had spent thirteen years wandering the world, and I was done with picking everything up and changing locations. Our oldest daughter was entering the eighth grade, and for educational reasons, I felt it was too hard on her to move. But that all changed when my husband's company moved locations. It was announced one day that we couldn't stay in Oklahoma any longer. The operation left. The next thing I knew, we were dragging our suitcases off the baggage claim in Beijing, China.

Once there, we fell in love with life in China. It was exciting, and the school was great. We made lots of new friends, and we found an international church.

There is a saying in international life: "Don't hang that last picture on the wall, because as soon as you do, the company will know you are settled, and then they will transfer you in a flash." Well, I hung that last picture, I'm afraid. The company promised that we could spend at least three years in China and our oldest daughter could finish out her senior year in Beijing International School. But then, the China business climate became very unpredictable, and the company wasn't getting its promised work. All international companies were suffering the same predicament.

Then, SARS (severe acute respiratory syndrome) struck, and that was the death knell for most of the international crowd. The bad business climate combined with the virus made all our lives difficult, and the international community began moving out, quickly thinning to a skeleton crew. We were moved to Denver, Colorado. Beijing, China, became just a memory.

In Genesis chapter 5, that dispersal happened very rapidly to the godly line of Seth. The godly line of Seth increased and they knew what was right, and then "boom," people's downhill rebellion deteriorated to one righteous person, Noah. The righteous died and their children didn't believe God. None of the godly line moved to another location, as we did in China, but the faith and belief in God diminished to one solitary person. In Genesis 6:9, it says Noah "walked with God." What is righteousness? _____
(Genesis 15:6)

If you have a Bible timeline you can see that Seth was probably alive when Noah was born and died a few years after Noah's birth. (I recommend Rose Publishing Bible Time Line booklet) Noah knew God, and someone must have told him about God. Could it possibly have been Seth?

Let's look at the condition of the earth after 1,600 years from Adam's sin to Noah. Genesis, Chapter 6, gives us a look at the destruction of sin on the world.

Genesis 6:4b: "There were _____ on the earth in those days, and also afterward when the _____ came in to the daughters of men and bore children to them. Those were the mighty men who were of old, men of renown".

The "sons of God" would be the part of creation that was a direct creation of God. In other words, "sons of God" didn't have mothers. Only Adam as a human qualified as a "son of God". (Read Luke 3:38) Angels were direct creations of God so they are called "sons of God". Those fallen angels/sons of God cohabited with human women and corrupted the human line. Jude 6 also told us that "angels left their first estate" which meant taking on human form to mix with the human race.

Genesis 6:11: The earth was _____.

Genesis 6:13: The earth was filled with _____.

For Further Study: *Interesting read about ancient people's accomplishments. "We Are Not the First: Riddles of Ancient Science" by Andre Tomas. This book gives a glimpse into what advancements were made before the flood. Since all the history of the time before the flood was washed away, we are not sure what state of development the world was in.*

DAY 3

ARK INSTRUCTIONS

Read Genesis 7 and 8

A few years ago, my daughter and I went to New Orleans for a basketball tournament. We had some free time in between games, and we were interested in how New Orleans was doing since Hurricane Katrina had devastated the city in 2005.

We jumped on a guided bus tour through the city. We saw the impact from the destruction of the hurricane winds and waters and also how the levees had been breached. Our tour guide told us that when the levees broke, the threat of the hurricane was already over. New Orleans residents thought they had made it through the hurricane and its effects. Some people were out barbequing steaks. Others were outside, enjoying the sunshine. Others, after being inundated with so much rain and flooding, had started the cleanup.

Our guide told us about the nuns on their knees, praying that bright morning at the moment the levees breached. As they were kneeling, they felt their feet getting wet. They jumped up and ran for the stairs to get to the second floor of the church. They barely made it. The water rushed in so fast and furiously, they almost didn't get up the stairs in time. A man barbequing on his deck looked up from his grill and saw a wall of water coming toward him. He too turned and ran and barely made it up on top of his roof. Others didn't make it, sad to say. It just happened too fast.

That was how it happened for those unrepentant people caught up in the flood. There wasn't time to run for the ark. The fountains of the deep broke open, and the floodwaters surged up (Genesis 7:11). Was the LORD patient with the people as they neared the time of the flood? _____(1 Peter 3:20). The LORD waited for them to change their minds while Noah and his sons built the ark. How old was Noah when the ark was completed? _____ (Genesis 7:6)

They must have enjoyed watching Noah and his sons building this "useless" boat. (Was there even a lake nearby?) I can imagine Noah and his sons were probably a spectacle that made many chuckle at as they watched the ark being constructed.

My dad was a carpenter, who built many houses with my uncle. When they started building a house, a few people would show up periodically to witness their progress. Some wanted to give advice, but many just came for the entertainment of watching this new house materialize, little by little. That's how I imagine those people responding—talking, laughing, and getting "a kick out of Noah's madness." What was the general attitude of the population before the flood? (Matthew 24:38–39)_____
Reread Genesis 2:5–6. Had these pre-flood people experienced rain? _____

For More Information about pre-flood conditions: "The Greenhouse Effect and Pre-Flood Days" by Ronald L. Cooper of the Institute of Creation Research. Before rain fell the first time, there seemed to be a cloak of moisture around the earth that filtered the rays of the sun.

Noah's Ark Gives Us a Picture of the Gospel of Grace.

1. *One Door-*

   The ark had one door (Genesis 6:16).

Compare with:

One way to salvation (Matthew 7:13 NKJV): "Enter by the _____," and John 14:6, Jesus said, "I am the way and the truth and the life. No one comes to the Father except _____."

2. *Come*- (an invitation to be saved).

The LORD said to Noah and family in Genesis 7:1a NKJV: "_____the ark, you and all your household." He used the word "come" because He was inviting them inside for salvation and God was waiting inside.

Compare with:

Jesus said, "come" (John 6:37 NKJV). "All that the Father gives Me will come to Me and the one _____to Me I will by no means cast out."

3. *Sealed*-

The ark was sealed and coated with pitch. Pitch is the Hebrew word *kapar*, which means to atone (*at one* or reconciled with God) (Genesis 6:14). The pitch sealed the ark and saved Noah and his family.

Compare with:

Ephesians 1:13b NKJV: "you _____ with the Holy Spirit of promise."

4. *Wait*.

The LORD waited _____ days before He

shut the door (Genesis 7:10). After the LORD shut the door; the time of grace was over (Genesis 7:16). Noah and family were safe inside.

Compare with:

We wait patiently for Jesus to return and Grace is available to all. (Romans 8:25) "But if we hope for what we do not see, we _____."
One day Jesus will return and grace will be over. We wait. The door of Grace isn't closed yet.

5. _Up_.

After the flood, Noah and his family *left by the covering of the roof* (not through door they entered); they went *up* (Genesis 8:13).

Compare with:

We will go up to meet Jesus (1 Thessalonians 4:17 NKJV). "Then we who are alive and remain shall be _____ together with them in the clouds to meet the Lord in the air. And thus we shall always be with the LORD."

Isn't the Ark a wonderful illustration of grace? In Titus 3:5a, it said, "not by works of righteousness which we have done, but according to His mercy _____," The work of the cross, expressed the deep love of Jesus to all of us and like the Ark, we just need to enter the narrow door to salvation.

Fun Fact: *Scientists at the University of Leicester have discovered that Noah's Ark could have carried 70,000 animals without sinking if built from the dimensions listed in the Bible.*

DAY 4

STARTING OVER

Read Genesis 9

Starting over is a daunting experience. When my husband and I moved to Pakistan in 1986, I was a newlywed. I had grown up in a small town, filled with people I knew and loved. Pakistan was the opposite of what I had known for the first twenty-five years of my life. I knew no one. The culture was strange and foreboding to a novice like me. The Muslim call to prayer, blasted over a loudspeaker five times a day from a mosque across the street from our home, was unsettling. Pakistani people were all dressed in a tunic type of dress with the women often covered from head to toe. No one talked to me, nor did they seem to want to talk to me. I had never felt more ill at ease.

In Pakistan, they drove on the left side of the road, which was another new learning experience. Trying to find my way around Islamabad, the capital city, and returning back home was difficult. My husband often left for weeks at a time to go on location hours away from where we lived. I literally broke out in hives a few months after I arrived. Starting our married life in that foreign land was hard, but Noah had a bigger task ahead of him.

I think of Noah and his family, disembarking the ark. The world had changed and they had to start over from scratch. Their relatives, aunts and uncles, nieces and nephews, all washed away. Their favorite restaurants and shops were all gone. Here are some more of the changes:

- o The climate was harsh; seasons began (Genesis 8:22—farming methods had to change)
- o Rain was now a part of their lives; flooding and droughts are now a factor
- o Capital punishment was instituted (government; Genesis 9:6).
- o Animals have a _____(Genesis 9:2).
- o They can eat _____ (Genesis 9:3—changed from only "green herbs" to eat in Genesis 1:29).
- o Don't eat _____ (Genesis 9:4).

I think of how they must have felt, thankful and yet bewildered. Have you had an experience of starting over? _____

Lets contrast the instructions given to Adam and Eve and how God changed some of them with Noah and family as they emerged from the Ark.

Adam and Eve- Genesis 1:28
"Then God blessed them and God said to them, Be fruitful and multiply; fill the earth, and subdue it; have _____ over the fish of the sea, over the birds of the air, and over every living thing that moves on the earth."

Noah and family-Genesis 9:1
"So God blessed Noah and his sons, and said to them: Be fruitful and multiply, and fill the earth."

Dominion is left out. Who has dominion over the earth, right now? Read 2 Corinthians 4:4 to see who is the god of this age. _____

In Matthew 4:8-9, Satan offered the kingdoms of the world to Jesus. Was it his to give? _____ Jesus said in John 12:31 "Now is the judgment of this world; now the ruler of this world will be cast out. Who is the ruler of this world? _____

These next references are future tense. In Daniel 7:11-12 it said the beasts (demonic entities) had their _____ taken away from them (at the end of the Tribulation). And a few verses later it said in Daniel 7:14-"Then to Him(Jesus) was given _____ and glory and a kingdom," Psalm 72:8 said "He shall have _____ also from sea to sea," Revelation 5:1-10 told us how the scroll (earth's mortgage) will be redeemed (called in) by the Lamb. Revelation 11:12 told us that in the future Tribulation time, after the seventh trumpet is sounded, it said, "The kingdoms of this world have become the kingdoms of our Lord of His Christ, and He shall reign forever and ever!" Dominion will then be returned to Jesus.

When did Adam and Eve lose dominion over the earth? _____ Why didn't Jesus call in the redemption of the earth at the cross and resurrection? Why is He waiting? _____

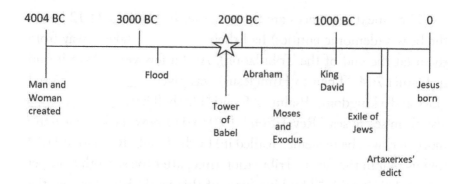

DAY 5

TOWER OF BABEL

Read Genesis 10 and 11

Noah and his family left the ark and started over. They knew the score. The LORD had destroyed the earth because of worldwide corruption and violence. "Let's not mess up again," they probably thought as they started anew.

After Noah left the ark, he started farming. He grew a vineyard and got drunk. A very strange event occurred when he was drunk. His son, Ham, entered his tent and "saw _____ of his father" (Genesis 9:22). "Uncovering your nakedness" is used in the Bible in other places. In Leviticus 18:6, "uncovering nakedness" is to have sexual relations with someone. In Genesis 9:24, Noah awakened from his drunkenness and knew what Ham had "done to him." It was more than just a look. Something happened.

Because Ham "saw the nakedness of his father," his son, _____, (Genesis 9:18 and 25) was cursed. Not

Ham but his son! Two hundred years later, after Canaan's children settled in Sodom and Gomorrah, God rained down fire and brimstone on those cities because of the sin of homosexuality. Could the sin of homosexuality and perversion have followed the cursed Canaan? _____

To follow that same thought, four hundred years later, Abraham, while living in Canaan, specifically mentioned that the _____ among whom he was living was not a suitable people to provide a wife for his son Isaac (Genesis 24:3-4). Abraham made his servant swear not to take a woman for Isaac from the Canaanite people. Seems to be a pattern here. What do you think? Could Canaan have had the same homosexual desires as his father Ham had, and Canaan's grandchildren continued that trend and Abraham was aware of that? _____ (Also, Abraham's grandson, _____, married a Canaanite woman, and that displeased his father, Isaac, in Genesis 28:6–9.)

But this event concerning Ham and Noah, revealed sin was still strongly present. The eight members of Noah's family experienced the ark and the flood, and they knew how seriously God judged sinfulness and rebellion. Even so, sin entered their lives and took hold of them. Probably since there were only eight people left on earth, Satan concentrated all his evil efforts on them.

But now, two hundred years passed, the generations of Noah's sons, Ham, Shem, and Japath, were not walking with God. In fact, they were constructing the _____ (Genesis 11:4-8) to thumb their noses at God, showing complete utter rejection of their Creator, again and didn't want to be "scattered abroad over the face of _____". (Genesis 11:4b) What would be the advantage of sticking together? God told us in Genesis 11:6b "now nothing that they _____ will be withheld from them". This tower was built to defy God's instruction to Noah to "fill the earth" or spread out. Spreading out would function to slow evil.

I've heard some thoughts on possible reasons they built the Tower of Babel. They may have built the Tower of Babel to be high enough so if God sent another flood, it couldn't come along and wash everyone away. Or another thought is that if this was a ziggurat type of tower, it's construction looked like steps, and they were demanding God to come down. And He did come down. Genesis 11:5 said "But the LORD _____ to see the city and the tower which the sons of men had built." Genesis 11:7 said, "Let _____ and confuse their language, that they may not understand one another's speech." After reading the above verse, was it more than one of the Godhead that came down? _____

My first trip to Thailand was in 1987. We had lived in Pakistan for a year, and we were ready for a vacation. On our way home to the USA, we toured Bangkok, Thailand. We signed up for a river tour that went through the Bangkok floating markets. The most remarkable sight for me on that tour was the Grand Palace, where the king of Thailand resided. When we visited that year, the palace roof had newly reapplied gold leaf, and it was brilliant and golden in the summer sun. The palace literally shimmered. We floated by and couldn't take our eyes off of it. That is how I imagine the Tower of Babel looked. Shining on a hill, maybe not gold but a brilliant white. I can imagine all the proud workers and people visiting, admiring its construction. They may have thought, *we are really a remarkable bunch. Look what we have accomplished! We don't need God.*

Now what? In Genesis 11:9, told us that the LORD _____ and scattered them. Can you imagine showing up at the Tower of Babel construction site the day after and your foreman couldn't communicate with you any longer because he spoke a different language? You went home in frustration and then tried to speak to your neighbors and they too, are speaking gibberish?

One of our first dinners overseas was a large mix of internationals in the Holiday Inn in Islamabad, Pakistan. There weren't any other English speakers of the twenty-five people who arrived that evening. We sat around a large table enjoying a meal together. Most of the internationals sat with their fellow countrymen, speaking their native languages together. Mark and I sat down and wondered what we should do. We couldn't communicate with any of these Middle

Eastern people. We didn't speak any of the languages that we heard at the table.

As the night wore on, the entire group kindly changed their communication to only English, to accommodate us. We were very grateful. It was a lonely feeling to hear so many different tongues and laughter and not be able to join in. I think if those kind people hadn't chosen to speak English that evening, we would have eaten quickly and left early. Confusing the language of those people at the Tower of Babel made everything hard and made them scatter from each other, it was more than making them uncomfortable.

After the flood, the population began with one righteous man and his family who knew and walked with God. Only two hundred years later after the flood, the rebellion occurred concerning the Tower of Babel. Everything was off the rails again. Adam was long gone. Noah (Genesis 9:28) was still around but he had faded out of the picture. Canaan was cursed, and there wasn't anyone who could be the witness for the LORD. In Isaiah 43:19–21, God said, "Behold I will do a new thing; now it shall spring forth: shall you not know it?" In verse 21, God says, "This people have I formed for Myself; they _____."

God had a new plan, a new witness for Himself. Now, Abraham will enter the stage! The genealogy of Abraham is given at the end of Genesis 11, the beginning of God's newly chosen people.

Lesson 2-Review

Who killed Abel?

_____

What was the name of the godly third son of Adam and Eve that began a godly people?

_____

Many years later, only one righteous person was left on earth. What was his name?

_____

What was built for the eight people to survive the flood?

_____

What were the names of the sons of Noah?

_____

Two hundred years after the flood, what tower was built?

_____

What was the purpose of this tower, and how did God respond?

_____

Notes

Notes

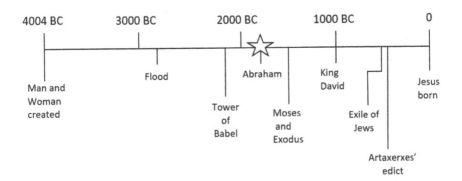

Lesson 3

GOD CHANGES HIS APPROACH— HE SELECTS A PEOPLE

Have you heard the phrase "We have always done it that way"? The manner something was done for a long time and has become the way everyone is comfortable doing it.

When we lived in other countries, I came home for the summers. I always enjoyed attending my childhood church. One summer, my mom asked me to help her with a ladies' morning Bible study group that the group had asked my mom to set up. The women emphasized to her that she could do anything she liked. It was completely up to her. I had always thought rearranging the serving tables differently in the church's fellowship hall would be advantageous, so Mom and I decided that since we were in charge, we would do that. The night before the Bible study was scheduled to meet, we went to the church and spent a good amount of time, decorating and rearranging.

When we returned the next morning, everything was undone. We stood there, realizing all our efforts that had been in futility. When one of the ladies briskly walked out of the kitchen, we mentioned that our setup had been completely changed. She looked at us in surprise and said, "Oh, we have always arranged the tables in this way! We changed it back." She whisked away, giving us no other explanation than that.

Now the LORD changed his method of reaching men. He was going to select a people for his name. God had dealt with people on earth as a whole for 2000 years. The rejection of God at the Tower of Babel caused God to select a man named Abraham who would be the start of a new nation as His witness. This Jewish nation was eventually going to come under the law, write the scriptures and provide a Savior.

Here are some questions to check on the Rose Publishing Bible timeline that you may purchase or access online.

o   Could Abraham possibly have known Noah? _____
o   Could Abraham and Isaac have crossed paths with Shem? _____

Both Noah and Shem could give firsthand accounts of the flood and the LORD's faithfulness. But they will soon be gone. Now God raised up a people for his name. Was there ever a time on earth that no one knew who God was? _____

DAY 1

CHOOSE ME

Read Genesis 12

Growing up, our neighborhood was full of children. I was the second to the youngest child in this group, I was always picked dead last for any softball game or activity some older kid was organizing. I had a strong desire to be one of the first chosen for anything. Usually, we younger ones felt fortunate to be included by those older kids. But one sunny day, I had gotten a very large pack of gum and was sitting on the curb when they began choosing teams for softball on the street in front of me. The same two boys would always choose teams. One was my cousin, who ordinarily chose anyone but me. This time though, he got an eyeful of my twenty-piece pack of gum.

He said to me, "If I pick you, will you pass out your gum to our team?" I nodded yes, and I jumped up and joined as the first-picked of my team. All my gum was given up to my team members as they were chosen. Soon, nothing was left of my gum, just the empty wrappers. Was I upset by the complete loss of my gum? Not in the least! I was one of the first picked, and I felt proud. The youngest, the smallest was chosen first. It felt great!

When the LORD chose the Jews to be His people, He didn't choose them because they were the largest group. In Deuteronomy 7:7, the LORD told the Jewish people, "You were the _____ of all peoples" What was another reason the Lord chose the Jewish people? (Deuteronoomy 7:8) _____

What about the Gentiles (non-Jewish people), were they rejected by God?

Did God beginning at Genesis 12 and onward in the Old Testament reject the Gentiles? No, actually The Tower of Babel was a rejection of God by the Gentiles. Just the opposite! (It's been said most all of the world's religions had their start at the Tower of Babel.)

Beginning from Genesis 12 to Acts 7 the Bible was primarily written to the Jewish people. Gentiles/non-Jews were rarely included. The Gentiles were also left out of the Abrahamic, Mosaic and Davidic covenants and the Gentiles didn't share these covenants until after Christ's Resurrection. (Ephesians 2:12)

Did God ignore the Gentiles? Here are some of the examples of God reaching out to the Gentiles in the "Jew only" times in the Old Testament.

1. When the Israelites/Jews left Egypt, there was a "_____" (Exodus 12:38) that were Egyptians and others who recognized the one true God and joined the Jews in the Exodus.
2. God sent a reluctant Jonah to preach to the people of Gentile city of _____. (Jonah 3:3)
3. Elijah was sent to a foreign widow in _____ (modern day Lebanon). Luke 4:26 and 1 Kings 17:7-16.

God is always in pursuit of all who want to come to Him. Martin Luther called God "the Hound of Heaven", because of God's tenacity. In 2 Peter 3:9b it said God is "_____that any should perish but that all should come to _____." God was and is interested in the Gentiles/non-Jewish people. But for now in this time period between Genesis 12 through Acts 7, He used this Jewish nation to accomplish His purpose of reaching everyone.

DAY 2

CALL OF ABRAHAM- THE FATHER OF THE JEWISH PEOPLE

Read Genesis 12

Let's take a look at Abraham's family members. Only Abraham received God's call. But initially, Abraham's father, Terah, and nephew, Lot, accompanied Abraham and his wife Sarah. (I want to emphasize that Abraham and Sarah are "one flesh" in God's eyes; anything told to Abraham was also for Sarah.) Here are some verses that round out the picture of each person of Abraham's family. Write the characteristics of each person.

Terah: (father of Abraham and Sarah): Joshua 24:2 _____
Sarah: (Sarai): Genesis 20:12 _____
Lot: 2nd Peter 2:7–8; Genesis 13:5 _____

Why do you think Lot and Terah go with Abraham when only Abraham was called? _____
   I suspect Terah felt he should go since he was at that time the patriarch of the family. Sarah was his only daughter, and usually, a daughter stayed with her parents. (When we learn what happened later on after Terah died, it's understandable that she needed the protection!)
   Terah's other son, _____, Lot's father, died sometime

before they left Ur. (Genesis 11:28) Lot inherited his father's wealth. Lot probably knew he could be a potential heir of Abraham and Sarah, who were childless. It was in his best interest to stay with his uncle Abraham and grandfather Terah.

Nahor, Abraham's other brother, who married Lot's sister, _____, (Genesis 11:29) stayed put in Ur. Nahor's family will provide marriageable cousins later on for Isaac (Abraham's son) and Jacob (Isaac's son). The family tree below shows how they were all interrelated.

It would be another four hundred years before the LORD instructed the Israelites *not* to marry their sisters and close relatives (Leviticus 18:11). Before and for some time after the flood, it was perfectly acceptable to marry a half-sister.

Family tree of Abraham and Sarah

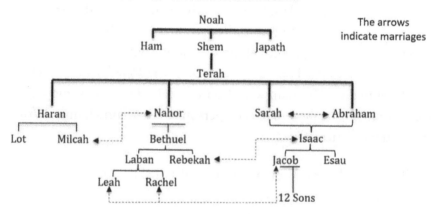

Have you ever not wanted to leave a beautiful place because you knew very few locations were comparable? My cousins owned a large lakefront cabin with all the bells and whistles in Minnesota. While visiting, we awoke to the soft sound of lapping waves and sunshine streaming through the big windows. Our wonderful aunt would have a pancake breakfast waiting for us. After breakfast, we would scamper to the long dock, where my uncle had the motorboat started and ready to take us for a ride.

While on the boat with my uncle, I loved how the wind blew

through my hair, how the sun warmed my skin while we munched on potato chips and sodas. We got to try our luck with water skis and water toys, but eventually, the day came when my dad packed up our car and our stay was over. I didn't want to leave that comfortable place.

That's how I imagine Sarah and Abraham might have looked at leaving beautiful Ur and beginning a nomadic life on a dusty road to a place that was almost sure to disappoint. Living in tents and packing and unpacking, tending of animals and no more familiar restaurants and shops. They traveled about six hundred miles from Ur to city of Haran and then made a long stop—twenty-five years, to be exact. After Terah (Genesis 11:32)_____, Abraham and Sarah continued on to the land God had promised which was an additional 400 miles.

Fun Fact: The city of Ur was a wealthy, populous, sophisticated pagan center of southern Mesopotamia, two hundred miles southeast of Bagdad. Its most prosperous era was during the time of Abraham.

Abraham was a wealthy man with a lot of livestock and servants. It had been an immense responsibility to get that group to the city of Haran. Now Abraham was faced with the task of moving all of them again to the land of Canaan. Abraham was _____years old (Genesis 12:4) when he led them on to a new land.

Chronology of Abraham's Life (Sarah is 10 years younger)
50: Terah, Lot, Sarai, and Abraham leave Ur to Haran.
75: All depart from Haran (Terah died).
100: Birth of Isaac.
140: Marriage of Isaac to Rebekah.
160: Birth of Jacob and Esau.
175: Death of Abraham.

DAY 3

THE TOPSY-TURVY WORLD
OF ABRAHAM AND SARAH

Read Genesis Chapters 13–19

Abraham and Sarah's next twenty-five years are covered in the chapters of 13-19. They already have been through a few trials, one of them being that Sarah hadn't conceived. In the chronological chart above, you see that Isaac was finally born when Abraham was one hundred years old!

These next twenty-five years was when all the action happened. First of all, Sarah's father was dead. Her protector was now gone. Sarah was beautiful but has been unable to produce an heir. I can imagine the gossip of the people around her. Abraham's wealth required that they designate an heir. They had chosen _____ (Genesis 15:2). But it was painful. Abraham and Sarah both wanted a biological heir, one that they produced together. The LORD had promised a great nation among other promises to come from Abraham. How could that happen if they didn't have a son or daughter?

After their move from Haran, they found their new location in Canaan was consumed by _____. Abraham and Sarah traveled to _____ for relief from the famine (Genesis 12:10).

This was where it got dicey. Sarah was beautiful, and Abraham knew that Pharaoh would probably want her in his harem, so Abraham came up with a plan for Sarah to say she was his _____ (Genesis 12:11–13). It was a half lie. Sarah agreed, and as Abraham suspected, Pharaoh saw Sarah and took her to his palace. Abraham benefited from Sarah being taken and gained wealth from Pharaoh. What did Abraham gain? (Genesis 12:16) _____

Sarah went with the Egyptians. What did Sarah lose? She lost her family, country, and husband. She likely didn't speak the language and would soon be violated by Pharaoh. What did this tell us about Abraham? _____

The LORD rescued Sarah by (Genesis 12:17), sending _____ upon Pharaoh. (This was a foretaste (Exodus 12:40–42) of what would happen four hundred years later when the LORD would rescue Moses and the nation of Israel from Egypt.)

Pharaoh sent Sarah back to Abraham. Pharaoh was very upset by Abraham's lies and then deports Abraham and family (Genesis 12:10–20). Whew! They dodged a bullet, didn't they? How do you think they felt? _____.

Was this a learning moment for Abraham? *Not really*. It happened again later on.

Have you ever had a super busy year? Abraham and Sarah were about to have a year that changed everything. We had a year like that. Our daughter's wedding was in 2019, the same year my husband and I built our home in North Dakota while trying to sell our home in Houston. We flew and drove back and forth, keeping our home on the market in Houston as well as trying to keep abreast of the building deadlines in North Dakota. It was frantic at times, and I felt we were drowning with details to take care of. I am glad to report that all of it got done and our daughter had a beautiful wedding. But the immense relief we felt was so sweet when our Houston home was sold, our North Dakota home was mostly built, and our daughter was married.

For your information: Sarah's Egyptian maidservant, _____, (Genesis 16:3) was given to Abraham, by Sarah, to give them a child. She conceived and had a son named _____ *(Genesis 16:11). It's highly probable that Hagar was acquired in Egypt and was part of the Pharaoh's gift given to Abraham in exchange for Sarah a few years prior.*

Fun Fact: *The Code of Hammurabi is a good reference to know how the ancients conducted themselves for childlessness and other social problems. Sarah seemed to be following this code of laws. The Code allowed a childless couple to take a maidservant to bear a child for them. The child was given to the wife to raise as her own. This was not done in Hagar's case. Ishmael remained Hagar's son. How old was Abraham at Ishmael's birth?* _____ *(Genesis 16:16)*

Abraham and Sarah's busy year ended with a miracle. In Genesis 17:1, we are told that Abraham was _____ years old and Sarah was eighty-nine when they heard the news. The LORD told Abraham that Sarah would bear a child at this time next year. Shocking to say the least because Sarah was way too old and Abraham _____ at the idea of it (Genesis 17:17). Sarah also _____ when she heard of it. (Genesis 18:12) They named their son Isaac, whose name means "laughter."

Read Genesis Chapters 20–21
The busiest year of Abraham's life timeline

Age 99: They were told Sarah will have _____ that year (Genesis 17:16)
Age 99: Abraham _____all males in household (Genesis 17:23)
Age 99: Abimelech _____Sarah and God rescued her again (Genesis 20:2)
Age 99: Sarah became _____ during this year (Genesis 21:1-2)
Age 100: Isaac was _____ (Genesis 21:5)

Abraham's behavior was puzzling. He let Sarah be taken away *again*. This time, Abraham was aware that Sarah would soon have a baby later that same year (Genesis 18:13). He told Abimelech, king _____, just as was done years ago in Egypt, that Sarah was his _____ (Genesis 20:2). After Abimelech took Sarah to his

palace, God lets Abimelech know that he was "_____"
because he had taken Abraham's wife (Genesis 20:3). God rescued
Sarah for the second time. Abraham again collected _____
(Genesis 20:14), and then they left and returned to Canaan. After
they returned to Canaan, Sarah conceived.

Fun Fact: *Abimelech was the title of every Philistine king, similar to a
title of "president" or "pharaoh".*

Why do you think Abraham replicated his mistake? _____

How do you think Sarah felt as Abraham allowed her to be taken
the second time? (Genesis 20:2)

_____

DAY 4

ABRAHAM'S FAITH CONFIRMED

When we look at all the events that Abraham and Sarah encountered and how the LORD twice rescued Sarah, it's hard for me to imagine why the LORD chose Abraham. He had many flaws and made big mistakes, but isn't that the point? God chooses us in spite of our weaknesses and sinful actions. God loves each one of us, and He gave His Son, Jesus, to die for us and redeem us. All we need is faith, which is simply to believe what God says.

When our daughter was two years old, she loved to jump into her daddy's arms from the sofa or a chair. She would giggle with delight as she flew into Mark's strong outstretched arms. He faithfully caught her every time. She loved that game. But one morning, as he was rushing to go to work, he walked by Ashley and me in the kitchen. She was standing on a chair next to me as we prepared lunch. Mark walked by, his briefcase in one hand and coffee cup in the other. Ashley leapt without warning. She was so sure her faithful daddy would catch her. Mark dropped his briefcase and just barely caught her by the skirt of her little dress. She chortled with delight as usual, but her daddy had to sit down to catch his breath, recovering from her near drop on that hard tiled floor.

Abraham too had great faith. He knew the LORD was going to do what He promised. Let's look at the promises made by God.

The Covenant Promises Given to Abraham

1. <u>Land</u>. Genesis 15:18: "To your descendants I have given this land, from the river _____ to the great River Euphrates."
2. <u>Seed</u>. Genesis 17:6: "I will make you exceedingly fruitful; and I will make _____ of you, and kings shall come from you."
3. <u>Blessing</u>. Genesis 12:3b: "And in you _____ shall be blessed." How has the earth been blessed? _____

The following equation is used by two of my favorite Bible study teachers, J. Vernon McGee (*Thru the Bible*) and Les Feldick (*Through the Bible*). It sums up well what God requires from us. Just take God at His word. Nothing more.

Faith + Nothing = Salvation

DAY 5

THE SON OF PROMISE

Traveling to Israel was definitely worth it in 2014. My husband and I thought about canceling the trip. He had had surgery about three weeks prior to leaving, and we didn't know if he would feel strong enough. The trip went well, and he felt great.

Arriving there, feeling Israel's heat and looking at the sandy terrain, I wondered, *this is the Promised Land?* It didn't look very "promising." Being raised in a farming community, we tend to evaluate every soil we come across. Looking at Israel's soil, I wondered how they got anything to grow in that dry, yellow, rocky dust. The only greenery was a few scattered weeds here and there. Our Jewish guide explained to us that Israel doesn't receive much rainfall during the year. But remarkably, every year, the rainfall had been increasing just enough to provide water for all the new immigrants arriving nearly daily in Israel. They're also converting seawater into fresh water. They needed it!

This was not a piece of real estate I would want to buy. And yet, Israel is one of the most fought over pieces of real estate in the world.

When Abraham and Sarah lived there, it must have been a different climate. This piece of real estate had been promised to Abraham to become a great nation of his descendants. It started with this little miracle baby. It must have been a wonderful day when Isaac was born. Sarah must have felt ecstatic. With this birth, she would become the mother of a nation that God had promised Abraham and her years ago. Sarah at her advanced age as her belly grew larger and larger, must have been the talk of the village.

Ishmael was around fourteen years old when Isaac was born. What a game-changer newborn Isaac created for Hagar and her son.

For Further Thought:
Have you watched the movie, The Lion King? It illustrates why Sarah sent Hagar away in Genesis 21:8-9. After Isaac was weaned around 3-5 years old, he would be sent with Abraham to learn the business. That meant he would be out of Sarah's watchful eye. Sarah saw Ishmael _____ at Isaac, (Genesis 21:9) and she knew Isaac's birth had caused Ishmael to lose his first-born status and inheritance.

In the movie, The Lion King, a similar situation took place. Simba, a baby lion cub was born to King Mufasa and his lioness wife. Simba, simply by his birth, took the position of next in line to be king. His wicked uncle Scar was upset because his chance to be king was gone. Scar tried to murder Simba and King Mufasa, who both stood in Scar's way to the throne. Scar succeeded in murdering King Mufasa, but Simba escaped. Prior to that incident, no one sensed that Scar had bad intentions and because of that, Scar was able to lure King Mufasa and Simba into a dangerous situation.

Sarah asked that Ishmael and Hagar be sent away, it seemed harsh but God _____ with Sarah's request. (Genesis 21:12) Do you think Sarah could have had the a foreboding sense about Ishmael, that there was danger for Isaac? _____ (Isaac and Ishmael eventually reunited to _____ Abraham, 70 years later. Genesis 25:9)

What about Ishmael?

Read Genesis 22

Ishmael was Abraham's son by Hagar, the Egyptian maid born fourteen years earlier. Wasn't Ishmael really the firstborn son? _____ Let's take a look.

In Genesis 22:2, God said, "Take now thy son, _____ Isaac". How can God say that when elder half-brother Ishmael was Abraham's son as well?

Think back in Genesis 1 and 2, when Adam married his wife, and they became "one flesh"? Before God, they, as husband and wife, literally were considered one body. There was only one person who was the other half of Abraham. That was Sarah. Only she could produce a son that was completely Abraham's. If Abraham and Sarah had adopted Ishmael, then Ishmael would have been Abraham and Sarah's son. But that didn't happen. Hagar had raised Ishmael, as her own son.

Abraham questioned God about Ishmael (Genesis 17:18) and God replied in Genesis 17:19, "No, _____ shall bear you a son and you shall call his name Isaac; I will _____ with him for an everlasting covenant and with his descendants after him."

Isaac was the promised son, the son of Sarah. This illustrated again the importance of the marriage covenant of "one flesh" in God's eyes.

Faith

Hebrews 11:6: "But without faith it is impossible to please him."

My husband worked for an oil service company for more than thirty years. We had a lot of faith in his company. While we lived overseas, our management assured us that if anything threatening happened politically or medically, every one of us would be flown out immediately. That gave us a lot of comfort. I felt safe and well taken care of, and we had complete confidence.

The day came in 1988 when this promise was tested. At that time, we lived in Islamabad, Pakistan, and one morning, we awoke to missiles flying all over the city. Hundreds of missiles were whistling all around us. When they hit, it was sudden. It would have been impossible to dodge any incoming missile. Luckily, the missiles weren't armed and didn't explode when they hit the ground, but nonetheless, the missiles' impact left huge craters.

My parents were visiting us at that unfortunate time, and they were at our home. After awakening to this dilemma, we thought it best to sit outside of the house on the patio. We felt that if a missile hit our concrete home, the house would likely cave in on top of us.

Every few minutes, we would hear the sound of an incoming missile, and my mom and I would stand up and start moving frantically around. Our Pakistani cook periodically came out of the house exclaiming in a high-pitched voice, "India is attacking, India is attacking!"

My dad, on the other hand, stayed seated, reading his newspaper, and didn't even flinch at the surrounding noise. Finally, I sat down in exhausted defeat and observed Dad's calm demeanor. I said to him, "How can you sit there like that?"

My dad lowered his newspaper slightly, peered at me over the page, and said, "This is your first war, isn't it?"

Mom and I started laughing, which broke our panicked mindset. There sat my dad, a two-time Purple Heart World War II veteran. He had been through all this before. He understood that if we were hit, we wouldn't have any foreknowledge of it. We would be toast. We calmed down and waited for it to end.

When it was over later in the day, the international crowd wanted to get out of Pakistan as fast as possible. Frantic calls were being made to secure a jet, and we were waiting for word of a jet to come pick us up. No jet ever came. The airport was closed, its tarmac riddled with craters left over from the ammo dump explosion. We were stranded.

Many weeks later, when we could have left, we didn't. Life had gone back to normal, and I continued on teaching and my husband working for the company. But we did lose that faith that the company could save us. Not that they had bad intentions, but they couldn't perform miracles to get us out of there. They had limitations.

But God performs miracles. He is in complete control. He has no limitations. He provided Abraham and Sarah their promised son, Isaac. God also provided another Son two thousand years later, God's only Begotten Son, and the Savior of the world, to make the sacrifice for our sin.

Read Hebrews 11:17–19 for a beautiful description of Abraham's faith and his knowledge that God would provide another sacrifice or that God would raise Isaac _____. Other scriptures of Abraham's faith are Genesis 15:6, Acts 7:2-8, Galatians 3:6-9, and James 2:23. Read these scriptures and describe Abraham's faith. _____

Abraham's obedience to God was displayed when he was told to sacrifice Isaac at Mount Moriah. This Biblical story demonstrated Abraham's faithfulness. See the following chart that compares Jesus' sacrifice with Isaac's near sacrifice.

Isaac and Abraham pointed to Christ's Future Sacrifice-Consider the similarities.

Jesus	Isaac
God's Only Begotten Son	Abraham's only son
Triumphal entry, rode on donkey	Saddled a donkey for trip

Location of both sacrifices

Calvary/Mount Moriah	Calvary/Mount Moriah

Other similarities

Carried wooden cross on back	Isaac carried wood on back
Three days in tomb	Three days travel
Two thieves crucified with Jesus	Two servants with Abraham

In Genesis 22:14, what did Abraham call that location? _____

Read Genesis 22:19. Why did the scripture mention only Abraham returned to the young men? Why wasn't Isaac mentioned? _____ Genesis 22:9-10 said, Abraham "*bound Isaac his son and laid him on the altar.*" Do you think Isaac resisted?

_____

Was Abraham faithful? _____

Food for Thought:

Talmudic Jewish sages taught that Isaac was thirty-seven years old at the time of the Mount Moriah sacrifice. (The Talmud is a collection of Jewish law and traditions.) The Talmud gave the reason for Sarah's early death was due to the reaction and angst of the possible sacrifice of her only son Isaac. How old was Sarah at the time of her death? _____ *(Genesis 23:1)*

After Sarah's death, Abraham married another wife named _____ (Genesis 25:1). Through her, Abraham gained another six sons, whose descendants became part of the Arab nations too.

Lesson 3 Review

Why did God select a people for His name?
_____

Did God give up on the rest of the world?
_____

Who was the faithful man called out to start a people/nation?
_____

Why wasn't Ishmael considered Abraham's first born?
_____

What were the three promises given in the Abrahamic Covenant?
_____

What was the significance of Abraham's near sacrifice of Isaac?
_____
_____

Notes

Notes

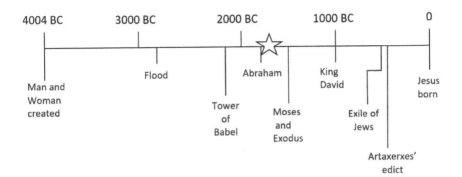

Lesson 4

THE REST OF THE STORY

Read Genesis chapters 23 and 24

I taught in an international school in Islamabad, Pakistan, for three years, from 1986 to 1989. My students were children from many different countries, whose parents were diplomats, residing in the capital of Islamabad, which was rich with a diversity of cultures. Most interesting for me, though, was getting to know Waheeda, my classroom aide. She was a beautiful Pakistani woman, very articulate and smart. Both of us were in our twenties, and we quickly became friends. She had a desk on the opposite side of my classroom. When the children would leave for "specials," such as PE or computers, we would always talk and enjoy each other's company.

In the second year of our three years teaching together, Waheeda got married. As was customary in Pakistan, her father arranged the marriage. She believed the man she was marrying was around thirty-five years old, a distant relative and seemingly a good choice.

I went to her wedding, staying on the women's side of the house, which was also the custom. Men and women didn't mingle. Waheeda met her husband for the first time on the third and final day of the wedding celebration. Her first glimpse of him was when they got into the same car to drive away as a married couple.

She told me later how shocked she was at seeing him. She had been adamant about not wanting a man more than fifteen years older than her. He was a least forty-five. Nothing about him seemed to match what she was told before the wedding. She felt betrayed. She struggled to accept this wedding and this man who was now her husband.

Isaac, Abraham's son, had an arranged marriage too, with a very different outcome. When Isaac saw Rebekah, he _____ her immediately (Genesis 24:67). This marriage is a beautiful illustration of Christ and the church and how we are His Bride. Let's compare Christ and His Bride and Isaac and Rebekah's marriage.

1. Abraham desired _____for his son, Isaac. Genesis 24:4
   God the Father desires _____for His Son, Jesus. Revelation 19:7-9

2. Abraham's servant, Eliezer (Genesis 15:2) was sent to find a bride. Genesis 24:2 (El=God, ezer=help)
   The Holy Spirit was sent after Christ's ascension to find souls for the Body or Bride of Christ. Acts 2:1-4
   The Holy Spirit is our _____. John 14:26a

3. Eliezer gave _____to Rebekah. Genesis 24:53
   Holy Spirit gives _____to the Bride of Christ at the moment we accept Jesus as our Bridegroom. 1 Corinthians 12: 4-11

4. Rebekah was asked if she would go with Eliezer to marry Isaac. She answered "_____." Genesis 24:58

The Holy Spirit seals each believer the Bride of Christ when we say yes. Ephesians 1:13-14

5. Isaac met Rebekah in the _____ (not his home). Genesis 24:65
   Jesus will meet His Bride in _____ (not in Heaven). 1 Thessalonians 4:17

The marriage proposal is not forced on either Bride. They come willingly. Why must it be willingly? _____

You are now introduced to the family God was going to use to make a nation for His Name. This family was far from perfect. God will use them to show the world who He is. This nation started from one man and expanded to a large nation of people on a very bumpy road. Let's get started.

DAY 1

LOTS OF DRAMA

Read Genesis Chapters 25-27

Have you ever been someone's favorite? I had that experience in elementary school. Our music teacher often picked me for the lead part in operettas we performed. We had an operetta every year, and I was memorizing lines and songs all fall. I wasn't excited about it because I was a shy young girl and didn't enjoy the spotlight. But it did make me feel special. Being someone's favorite does give you a boost.

We will find that the patriarchs (Abraham, Isaac, and Jacob) played a lot of the "favorite card" in the narrative of the beginning story of the Jewish people.

Abraham's son, Isaac, and his wife, Rebekah, had twin sons named Esau and Jacob. They each had a favorite son. Isaac loved _____, and Rebekah loved _____ (Genesis 25:28). Even though Isaac and Rebekah had a strong marriage, there was more than a little friction between their children. Isaac and Rebekah's twins were very different individuals. Esau was not a spiritual person. He rejected his birthright as the oldest son and spiritual leader of the family by selling his birthright to his brother, Jacob, for a bowl of _____ (Genesis 25:29-34).

Jacob, the second-born of the twins, acquired the birthright and then schemed to get the double portion of inheritance from Esau as

well. Rebekah, his mother, aided and abetted Jacob. When tricky
Jacob succeeded, Esau _____ and Esau planned _____
his deceitful younger brother (Genesis 27:41). Jacob fled.

Do Esau and Jacob remind you of Cain and Abel? _____

Why did God leave Esau out of the lineage of the Jewish nation?
(Genesis 25:34, Hebrews 12:16) _____

For Your Information:
The firstborn would receive a double portion of the inheritance, and also he
became the spiritual head of the family. The firstborn would be in a special
covenant relationship with the LORD.

After fleeing from Esau, Jacob stayed with his Uncle Laban
who had two daughters. Later on, Jacob married the two daughters,
Rachel and Leah. Jacob's loved _____, the only woman he
wanted as his wife. (Genesis 29:18) (Read Genesis 29 to learn how
their father Laban deceived Jacob into first marrying Leah before
Rachel became his wife.)

Continuing the favoritism pattern, Jacob loved Rachel's children
more than Leah's children.

Rachel's son, Joseph, was Jacob's _____ (Genesis 37:3–4).
Jacob would eventually give Joseph firstborn son status (see Genesis
48:22) even though Joseph was the eleventh son of twelve brothers.
The coat of many colors, given by Jacob to Joseph, indicated Joseph's
favored position. The other ten brothers _____. (Genesis
37:4) The brothers acted upon their murderous, jealous thoughts
by _____. (Genesis 37: 12-36) Favoritism again was
causing problems.

Read Genesis chapters 30-50 that completed the story of Joseph,
and the entire family's transfer to Egypt. Those seventy people will
expand into a large nation in four hundred years while living in
Egypt.

As you can see, favoritism usually causes major difficulties.
What I love about the Bible is that it doesn't gloss over and make its

characters look good. The Bible tells the good, the bad, and the ugly. The Bible reveals the truth.

For Further Study

What was Jacob's name changed to? _____ (meaning "he wrestles with God")(Genesis 32:28) Jacob wrestled with the pre-incarnate Christ Himself one night. It was the evening before he was to meet up with his twin brother, Esau, for the first time since he fled from home.

In 2014, we visited the city of Hebron in Israel. Located in Hebron is the Cave of the Patriarchs. Jews and Muslims revere the cave because both groups claim Abraham as their father. Jews consider this site to be their second holiest site in the world, the first being the Temple Mount in Jerusalem. Both Jews and Muslims wrestle for access to this site.

The Jews call the Cave of the Patriarchs, the Cave of Machpelah. Abraham bought this cave as a burial site when Sarah died (Genesis 23:14–20). Who deeded it to Abraham? _____ The cave was used to bury Abraham and Sarah, Isaac and Rebekah, and Jacob and Leah. Where's Rachel, the favorite wife of Jacob? Why isn't Rachel buried in the Cave of the Patriarchs?

Rachel died and was buried in Ephrath (Bethlehem) immediately after giving birth to her second son _____ (Genesis 35:16–19). You can visit Rachel's tomb in Israel today in the hills of Judea where the lambs sacrificed in the second temple period were raised (1000 BC to 70 AD). Rachel's name means "ewe."

Leah (married first) was Jacob's wife in God's eyes. She was Jacob's other half. Jacob did not treat Leah as a traditional first wife should be treated during her lifetime, but after her death, she received "wife" status by being buried alongside Jacob in Hebron, in the Cave Of the Patriarchs (Machpelah) Genesis 49:31. Through Leah's son, ___, came the lineage of Christ (Genesis 49:10).

These sisters probably had a good relationship before their father

Laban tricked Jacob into marrying Leah even though he only wanted Rachel. Jacob married them both, but from that point on, Leah was considered second best. Rachel didn't want to share her husband and resented her sister. It must have been painful for both of them. Can you imagine how each of them felt? _____

Take a look at the following chart of which son/grandsons of Abraham produced the Jewish nation and which sons/grandsons produced Arab nations. Isaac was the son of Abraham whom the Jewish nation originated from and gained the promises of the covenants promised to Abraham. Only one of Isaac's sons, Jacob and Esau became part of the Jewish nation and came under the covenants. Which one? _____

Origins of the Jewish and Arab Nations

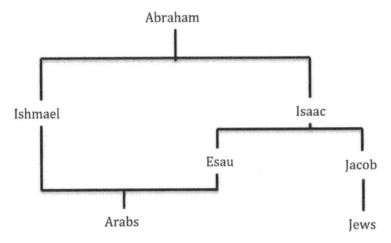

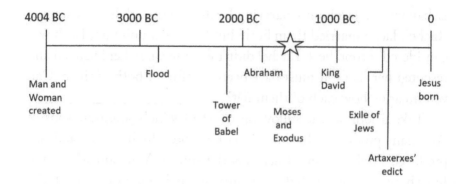

DAY 2

AN EGYPTIAN PRINCE
AND A VICE PRESIDENT

Read the book of Exodus

Cairo, Egypt, had the most snarled traffic I have ever seen. One evening, we got stranded on a six-lane road in the middle of the city. All traffic had come to a sudden stop. Cars all around us left their lanes and were nosing into small spaces as each driver tried to squeeze ahead and escape, which made everything much worse. We sat in the car with our Egyptian friends in the early evening heat, windows open and car turned off, waiting for the congestion to break and the flow to resume. Car horns blared as tempers flared, but our attention was diverted when our friends, Aladdin and Maiza, told us to look at the Cairo skyline. The sun was setting and spotlights were beginning to spectacularly light up the proud Pyramid of Giza. We thought of how those amazing pyramids were probably there when

Moses lived in the palace around 3500 years ago. Moses may have looked at those very same pyramids.

Egypt has played a large role in Israel's history. Remember how Abraham went to Egypt with Sarah and the Pharaoh deported them? That was the beginning of Israel and Egypt's relationship. Jacob and his family (which included eleven sons in all with a total of seventy members in the family) moved to Goshen, Egypt, when a dire famine occurred. Jacob settled there because his favorite son, Joseph, was second in command in Egypt (like a vice president). Joseph said in Genesis 50:19-20, "_____."

Those seventy people grew to a nation of millions in four hundred years. God told Jacob not to fear to go to Egypt, because He would make you a (Genesis 46:3)"_____." However, four hundred years later, Joseph had died, and the Israelites had lost their favored status. The Israelites had transitioned into a slave workforce, and the Hebrew/Israelite people were suffering. (Exodus 6:5) God had also promised Jacob in Genesis 46:4 that He would bring "_____." That now brings us to Exodus. God used a man named Moses, who would lead them out of Egypt.

Why Did God Use the Country of Egypt to Grow Abraham, Isaac, and Jacob's Descendants into a Nation?

Egypt was an economic power that could support Jacob's family of seventy persons that increased to a Hebrew nation of millions in four hundred years.

Egypt at that time developed from hieroglyphics to a phonetic system of writing. Was it possible that the Hebrews developed their own phonetic system of writing as they observed the Egyptian adoption of the Phoenician Alphabet? The Hebrews/Israelites were ready to receive the law at Mount Sinai after the Exodus from Egypt because of their ability to read.

God used Moses as the reluctant leader to rescue the sons and daughters of Abraham, Isaac, and Jacob. Moses, who was raised in the Egyptian palace as a prince, was Jewish by birth but adopted by the princess of Egypt. He had life going his way and Moses was "mighty in _____."(Acts 7: 22 NKJV). Then God called him to lead the Israelites out of Egypt. Moses was the man God had chosen and specially prepared for this moment. Moses was well educated but had one problem. What was that problem? (Exodus 4:10)_____

The Israelites rejected Moses the first time he tried to lead them out of slavery. The second time, forty years later, they followed Moses (Acts 7:27-35).

God instructed Moses to tell Pharaoh to "let My people go." (Exodus chapters 7:16) Pharaoh said no. Because of Pharaoh's refusal, God sent _____plagues upon Egypt. (Exodus chapters 7-11) After each plague, Pharaoh always refused to let the people go until the last plague occurred.

That last plague was called the "_____." (Exodus 12:5–12) The death angel *passed over* all the homes that had _____ on the front door posts. The blood was from a sacrificed lamb. In the homes that didn't have blood on the doorposts, the firstborn in each of those homes tragically died during the night. Pharaoh found his firstborn son dead. Read Exodus 12:29-30. Who and what was affected? _____ Then Pharaoh let the Israelites leave immediately while the Egyptian nation was rocked by anguish and death. What time of day did the Israelites leave (Exodus 11:4; 12:30-31)? _____

Pharaoh soon regretted his decision to let the Hebrews/Israelites leave and chased after them. Why did Pharaoh regret the Hebrew's exodus (Exodus 14:5)? _____

Moses parted the Red Sea and the Israelites passed through with the pursuing Egyptian army on their tail. Did the Israelites have to walk on a muddy seabed? Exodus 14:21-22_____
The water crashed in on the Egyptian army when they tried to cross after the Hebrews/Israelites had passed safely through (Exodus 14:26-28). How many of the Egyptians survived? _____

(Exodus 14:28) God's majesty and power was displayed through the supernatural ten plagues and the parting of the Red Sea.

The Passover was a significant prophetic event. The Israelites/Jews/Hebrews were told to observe the Passover every year since that time. They had been observing The Passover for one thousand five hundred years after they left Egypt until Christ came as the final Passover Lamb. How long were they to observe the Passover? _____(Exodus 12:24) Most Jews still observe it. We'll study the Passover in lesson 5.

This is an amazing story of God's power and might. The plagues were a building process that demonstrated how God is all-powerful and the only true God. Egypt had many gods they worshiped. The individual plagues often used one of those so-called gods against the Egyptians to persuade Pharaoh to let the Hebrews/Israelites go.

Do you think God was revealing Himself as the all-powerful God only for the Israelites? Exodus 7:5 _____ Besides the Israelites, did others hear of God's display of His Majesty years after the parting of the Red Sea? Read Joshua 2:9–11. _____

DAY 3

THE LAW/MOSAIC COVENANT

Arriving in Islamabad, Pakistan in 1986, we found Pakistan under martial law. Somber blue-suited policemen were on every street corner, waving people down, stopping cars at every stoplight. What was unusual was that the military police had no transport. None of them had a police car, motorcycle, or horse. Being merely on foot and unable to chase someone down for noncompliance to the law significantly diminished their power.

Our first interaction with these policemen occurred on our first day in Pakistan. Our friends picked us up and drove us from the airport to our new home. As we travelled, a policeman tried waving us over. Our British friend didn't stop. In fact, he sped up to get past the policeman who was frantically waving his hands at us. We lost sight of that uniformed man in our rear window as we sped away. Our friends then advised us never to stop when a policeman waved us over. When ordered to stop by the police, they said, "Just keep driving. They can't be trusted."

I couldn't comprehend that. Those uniformed men were the law. We must stop. Fortunately, martial law was lifted soon after I arrived. I was relieved. Disobeying the law went against all I knew.

The Hebrew/Israelite nation of people, traveling from Egypt to Mount Sinai, would soon be asked by God to come under the law. President Zia of Pakistan ordered martial law, which we temporarily lived under in Pakistan. He didn't ask anyone if they minded. Pakistan was placed under martial law by force. In contrast, God asked the Israelites, if they would come under the law (Exodus 19:8). What did they answer? _____ Let's define parts of the law that was given to Moses and the Israelites.

1. **Moral** Law/10 commandments- Exodus 20:1-17
Is eternal and shows the mind of God
2. **Civil Law**- Exodus chapters 21-40 (not in effect today)
Six hundred thirteen commands given for daily living
3. **Levite Law**- mainly the book of Leviticus (not in effect today)
The rules for priests and the administration of offerings

The Civil and Levite law were fulfilled by Jesus's death on the cross and resurrection. We are now under grace. Is the Moral Law or Ten Commandments in effect today? _____ Why did the Levite and Civil law end for the Jews at the resurrection? _____
We are still under the Moral law/Ten Commandments, except for the fifth commandment in Exodus 20:8 which was to worship on the Sabbath or Saturday. That worship day has now been changed to Sunday for most Christians, because that was Jesus' resurrection day. Here are some scriptures to explain why it changed.

Romans 14:5 "One person esteems _____ another; another esteems _____. Let each be fully convinced in his own mind."

Colossians 2:16 "So let no one _____ in food or in drink, or regarding a festival or a new moon or _____,"

1 Corinthians 16:2 and Acts 20:7 indicated that the early Christians were meeting on the _____ day of the week.

Romans 13:9 written by Paul gave a list of the commandments, but "keeping the Sabbath" was left off. Instead we are told, "not to _____ the assembling of ourselves together" in Hebrews 10:25. Notice there is no mention which day of the week is the day of worship. The liberty we experience under grace frees us in many ways.

We lived in Denver for around eight years. Whenever I exited the street where we lived, I had a beautiful view of Mount Evans. As I would start driving down the hill, Mount Evans loomed up in front of me. It was topped with snow, impressive and majestic. Seeing Mount Evans always made my day a bit brighter.

God used an impressive mountain called Mount Sinai to give His law to his people on the way to the Promised Land. This was a supernatural time for the Israelites. Besides the parting of the Red Sea, God provided a fire to lead the Israelites by night and a _____ by day (Exodus 13:21). They received _____ (Exodus 16:4) that fell from heaven to eat every day of the week except on the Sabbath. On Fridays, they took enough for the Sabbath because on the Sabbath there was _____. (Exodus 16:26.

God was with them. When they arrived at Mount Sinai (Exodus 19:2), something special was going to happen.

For Your Information:
Where is Mount Sinai? Walking the Bible by Bruce Feiler gives an insight into Mount Sinai's actual location, rather than the traditional location given in modern times. Bruce Feiler walked most of the geographical locations of the Bible. He concluded that Mount Jabal al-Lawz in Saudi Arabia is the actual Mount Sinai peak rather than the one that you find identified on maps today.

Picture this nation of people, all their livestock, and all their possessions, camped around the foot of Mount Sinai. They knew God was at work, and they were preparing for what God had for them.

God had demonstrated who He was through all the miracles He'd performed since they had left Egypt. What did the people witness at the foot of Mount Sinai? Read Exodus 20:18. _____

Here was what God said to his people, the Israelites, in Exodus 19:3–6 NKJV. "And Moses went up to God, and the LORD called to him from the mountain, saying, "Thus you shall say to the house of Jacob, and tell the _____: "You have seen what I did to the _____, and how I bore you on eagles' wings and brought you to Myself. Now therefore, if you will indeed obey My voice and keep My covenant, then you shall be a _____ to Me above all people, for the earth is Mine. And you shall be to Me a kingdom of _____ and a _____ nation.' These are the words which you shall speak to the _____."

To whom was God speaking? _____ Did God mention any other nation than Israel? _____ Did any Gentile nation ever come under the law? Malachi 4:4 said, "Remember the Law of Moses, My servant, which I commanded him in Horeb (Mount Sinai)_____, with the statutes and judgments." The Law was given to one nation of people, the Jews…no one else.

There also was a logistical part to keeping the law that Gentiles couldn't do. You needed either a temple or the Ark of the Covenant to fulfill the Levite part of the law. At times, it was geographically impossible to come under the law because you had to live close enough to make sacrifices _____year at the temple (Exodus 34:23). The Jews needed to travel to Jerusalem, where the temple was located. If you lived in China, India, well, you get the picture.

The law was intense. The book of Exodus has the law and the other books of the law are given below.

~ The book of **Leviticus** was given for instructions for the priests as they performed their sacrificial duties. (Levitical law)
~ The book of **Numbers** was given to list the tribes and the population of each.

~ The book of **Deuteronomy** was given after the 40 years of wandering in the wilderness. God reiterated the law again before the Israelites entered the Promised Land.

So what is the point of giving the law? No one can accomplish it. Why would a loving God go through all this trouble when it can't be accomplished? _____ Apostle Paul answered this best. Paul said in Galatians 3:24-25 NKJV, "Therefore the law was our _____ to bring us to Christ, that we might be justified by faith. But after faith has come, we are _____". Romans 3:20b said, "for by the law is the _____ of sin."

The law showed us we couldn't make ourselves good enough to enter the presence of God. We need Jesus, our Savior. The law was our "tutor." The law demonstrated/taught "There is none righteous, _____" (Romans 3:10). When did you realize you couldn't become good enough to get to heaven and that you needed a Savior? _____

In Exodus 24:3, after the LORD gave Moses the Ten Commandments and the Civil law, the Israelites again corporately agreed to come under the law, and they reiterated their answer of "We will do."

They ratified the covenant. It was like a marriage covenant with the LORD. In Jeremiah 3:14b NKJV, what did the LORD say to the nation of Israel about marriage? _____ Exodus 19 event was a marriage between God as the husband and Israel as His wife. In Isaiah 54:5, it beautifully depicted what relationship Israel now had with God when they said as a people, we will do it, "For your Maker _____, The LORD of hosts is His name;"

God was now the nation of Israel's husband. That would rock my world! Standing there at Mount Sinai, having witnessed all God's power and majesty and realizing God was like a husband! What happened next was surprising after the supernatural demonstration of the care God had exhibited to His people. We'll continue with the events in day 4.

After seeing God's power as Israel had, would you have had complete faith in Him? _____

DAY 4

DON'T MAKE ME GO!

Our children were born when we were abroad for thirteen years. Between transfers to a new country, we often stayed in hotels for months at a time. Arriving in Villahermosa, Mexico, we learned our house was not ready. We checked into a hotel, where we stayed for three months. We spent many hours of every day, swimming in the hotel pool. Our daughters learned to swim on their own at three and five years of age because of their constant exposure to the pool. They became fearless.

The only time I witnessed any fear from them in the pool was the first time they jumped off the high dive. They both begged to try it, but when they looked down, it was frightening. They hesitated. They looked down at their daddy in the water, assessing whether they should jump. Mark was assuring them he would be there to help them. They knew their daddy, and they put their faith in him and jumped. They loved it. Mark eventually regretted coaxing them to jump. He got tired of treading water under the diving board incessantly for the remaining months at the hotel.

The Israelite people knew God. He was faithful. God was strong and mighty. He miraculously rescued them in Egypt. And yet, they failed in a tremendous way.

After receiving the law, the Israelites traveled from Mount Sinai to Canaan's border, a place called Kadesh-Barnea. The Promised Land now lay right before them. God said in Exodus 23:20, "Behold,

I send an Angel before thee, to keep you in the way, and to bring you to the place _____" (Promised Land). What was the protection God told them He would give them in Exodus 23:28 as they entered the Promised Land? _____

It was theirs for the taking, but they refused to go. They said they wanted to return to Egypt. What were they scared of in the Promised Land (Numbers 14:3)? _____

God considered the Kadesh-barnea event very grievous. Hebrews 3:8-12 warned by using this event as the example, "Do not harden your hearts as in the rebellion, In the day of trial in the wilderness, Where your fathers tested Me, tried Me, and saw My works _____. Therefore I _____." How did God describe that generation in Psalm 95:10-11 that refused to enter at Kadesh-barnea? _____ Why was that generation's refusal to enter the Promised Land considered so grievous by God? _____

So now what? Having refused to go in, the Israelites had no options left. The Promised Land was this specific land in front of them. There were no substitutes. This land was promised to Abraham, Isaac and Jacob four hundred years ago. Because of their refusal, the Israelites would wander in the desert for forty years, until the generation that refused to enter had passed away. What does God tell them in Numbers 14:29? _____
When the Israelites go into the Promised Land forty years later, it is a much harder ordeal. There are no hornets to clear their way.

Do you think we would have reacted differently? _____

While in China, we had the opportunity to go with a group from our company to explore the part of the Great Wall that had not been restored. It was a long mountainous walk with no defined trail; the climb at times involving crawling up the side of a steep rocky grade, incurring a lot of scrapes and bruises. When I first heard about it, I wasn't excited. It sounded too difficult. I thought about the dangers, snakes and risks. Maybe someone in our group might fall. Then, how would we get that injured person back to safety? We would be in the wilderness.

We took on the challenge and we decided to go on that climb. The views were breathtaking. The winding, crumbling Great Wall stretched as far as the eye could see. We were so glad we joined up for that thrilling hike. I can still remember the spectacular views of that strenuous hike. It was an unforgettable experience, but there was risk involved.

I wonder if that was how those faithless people felt looking at the Promised Land stretching out before them. They were afraid to take the risk, causing them to miss more than a great view. That generation missed the land of milk and honey, the Promised Land. How many years later did the next generation enter the Promised Land? _____ (Deuteronomy 2:14)

For Your Information:

The Hebrews, Israelites and Jews are the same nation of people, called by different names. Early on, they are called "Hebrews", because their father Abraham was a Hebrew. "Israelites" refer to the nation after God changed Jacob's name to Israel and through Jacob's twelve sons began the twelve tribes of Israel that grew into a nation in Egypt. The third name "Jews", referred to the Southern Kingdom of Judah. King David and Solomon's kingdom divided into two kingdoms, called Israel and Judah. The name "Jews" comes from the nation of Judah.

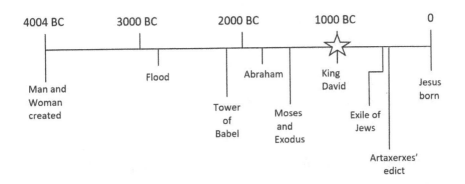

DAY 5

LONG LIVE THE KING?

My youngest daughter moved to Thailand to get her master's degree in mechanical engineering. We visited her in Thailand in 2019. We observed that Thai people are very respectful of their royal family.

Pictures of Thailand's king were plastered everywhere. Shrine-like stands with a large placard of the king or members of the royal family were at every major street corner. They were depicted wearing regal robes and sometimes a crown or two. The stands were well kept, and there was no graffiti on the placards.

At my daughter's Thai university, a stand for the king sat in the center plaza of her engineering building. Red plush curtains framed both sides of the placard, and vases with fresh flowers were placed there daily. The king smiled down at us as we ate lunch in the plaza.

No one in Thailand is allowed to say anything negative about the royalty. The king demands your respect, your taxes, and your devotion, whether or not you agree with his policies. The only escape from his rule is when he dies.

Read the book of Joshua for Israel's entry into Canaan, the Promised Land.

For Further Study:
The people of Israel were divided into twelve tribes. Each tribe descended from one of the sons of Israel/Jacob. The Promised Land was divided into portions by tribes. Joseph's portion was doubled since he received two portions because Jacob/Israel considered Joseph to be the eldest son. Joshua 16:4 said, "So the children of Joseph, _____ and _____ took their inheritance. (The tribe of Levi was not included but rather was given properties in certain _____ to dwell in when they weren't serving at the temple. (Joshua 21:3))

Read Judges and 1st and 2nd Samuel

When the Israelites arrived into the Promised Land, God set up government of a system of judges for a theocracy rather than a monarchy. At first, when Joshua was alive, the people stayed on track. Read Judges 2:7 for the reason the people served the LORD _____.
After Joshua died, the people angered the LORD. How did they do that? (Judges 2:11-15) _____Various judges ruled for over three hundred years after their arrival in Canaan. The Israelite people noticed that all the nations around them had kings. The elders of Israel demanded a king because of what reasons? _____ (1 Samuel 8:5)

The LORD told Samuel, (who was the final judge/prophet of Israel), in 1 Samuel 8: 7. He said, Give them a king, they are not rejecting you _____. Samuel warned the nation that a king would take much from them. What were some of those things? (1 Samuel 8:10-22) _____

God was being _____ (1 Samuel 10:19). The Israelites got their king. They came under the rule of men who might or might not have their best interests at heart. More importantly, would their kings listen to God? The scriptures revealed that very few of these kings did well.

King Saul was their first king. He was kingly in every way, like the stuff of romance novels—tall and good-looking. Saul, it will be revealed, lacked character. He was from the line of the tribe of _____. (1 Samuel 9:1)

Eventually, King David took King Saul's place. King David was from the tribe of Judah and was from what city? _____ (1 Samuel 16:4 and 13)

Read 1 Samuel 15:10-23. What was the event that ended King Saul's kingly line? _____ As you can imagine, King Saul wasn't happy about Samuel anointing David as future king. He tried to kill David by _____ (1 Samuel 18:10–12). David survived Saul's attempts to kill him and ran from King Saul for eight years to escape harm.

King David began the new kingly line that lead to another King named Jesus, Son of David, born in Bethlehem a thousand years later. Jesus, born of a virgin, the Son of God, will reign for a _____ in the coming Millennial kingdom and then forevermore. (Revelation 20:4b)

**Read 2 Samuel 7:8–16, for details of the <u>Davidic Covenant</u> God made with King David. God said in 2 Samuel 7:16a to David, "And your house and your kingdom what be established _____ before you. Your throne shall be established _____."
What a promise!**

King David's son _____ ruled after David died (1 Kings 2:10-12). His rule was the golden age for Israel. Read 2 Chronicles 9:22–28 and give some details of his reign. _____

God told King Solomon to build the amazingly beautiful first temple. When it was built, the priests brought the _____ (2 Chronicles 6:11) and placed into the temple. The Glory of the LORD filled the temple, which was represented by a _____ (2 Chronicles 5:13b-14). (The Glory of the LORD will eventually depart from the temple hundreds of years later, recorded in Ezekiel 10, because of Israel and Judah's idolatrous behavior.)

After Solomon died, there was a jostling of power for the throne. King Rehoboam, son of Solomon, began to rule but taxed the people at a very high rate. Read 1 Kings 12:4 and 13–15. What are King Rehoboam's words about taxation? _____

A rebellion occurred, and the kingdom split into two kingdoms. The original kingdom was called Judah, and the one that broke off was called Israel, with Jeroboam as their king. For the next hundreds of years, the former glory of Solomon's kingdom waned and diminished. The spiritual level ebbed and flowed for the kingdom of Judah, but the Kingdom of Israel's spiritual level was completely absent. Read 2 Chronicles 11:15 to see what the kingdom of Israel was worshipping rather than the LORD. _____ Who left the Kingdom of Israel and returned to the Kingdom of Judah? _____ (2 Chronicles 11:13-14) This led to many people from the ten tribes of the Kingdom of Israel to return back to the Kingdom of Judah.

King Saul (first king from tribe of Benjamin discontinued)

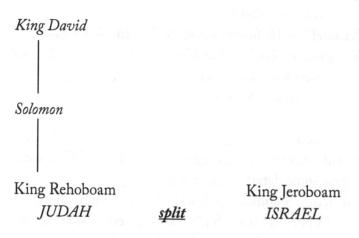

King David

Solomon

King Rehoboam   King Jeroboam
  JUDAH   *split*   *ISRAEL*

Summary of the Divided Kingdoms

1. *Kingdom of Judah/Southern Kingdom—began with King* _____ *(1 Kings 11:43)*

o Which two tribes stayed with Judah? (1 Kings 12:21)

_____

o Judah had the _____ which caused the Kingdom of Israel to fear their people would reunite with Judah. (1 Kings 12:26-27)

o Judah had a few good kings that followed the LORD.

o Judah was taken captive in 606 B.C. to _____ (2 Kings 25:10-11 and 21)

2. *Kingdom of Israel/Northern Kingdom—began with King _____ (1 Kings 12:20)*

o Ten of the tribes formed the kingdom of Israel.

o The kingdom of Israel did not have a temple. Their kings found new gods for their people to worship. Where did they worship? (1 Kings 12:28–31) _____

o The kingdom of Israel had all bad kings.

o Where was the Kingdom of Israel exiled in 722 B.C.? (2 Kings 17:23) _____

Many of the books of the Old Testament from the book of 1 Kings to the very last book of the Old Testament, Malachi, wrote of both kingdoms' rebellion against God. God sent prophet after prophet to both kingdoms, and most were rejected or killed. A lot of these books of the Bible after First and Second Kings and First and Second Chronicles are named after prophets that were active during the reigns of various kings from both kingdoms. God warned the kingdoms through these prophets that they would be judged. False prophets proclaimed, "All is well" to both kingdoms, and they often chose to believe the false prophets. In the end, both nations went into captivity. What was the practice that God lost patience with the kingdom of Israel and let them be carried away into captivity? _____ (2 Kings 17:17-18)

One hundred and fifty years later, the kingdom of Judah was carried into captivity. What was the name of Judah's last king? _____ (Jeremiah 52:11) After Judah was taken captive, the

_____ was destroyed (Jeremiah 52:13) and Jerusalem was desolate.

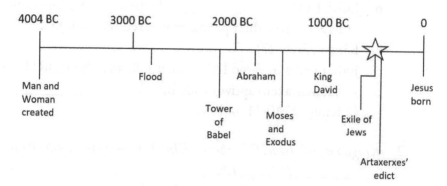

Now what? Did God give up on his people? Never! As always, God is faithful. God set a time clock for His people to determine when their Messiah/Redeemer/King was coming. After the final king of Judah, there would not be any other king on the throne. Their next King will be King Jesus, the Son of David, the Savior of the world. He was coming. Would they be ready for him?

The prophet Isaiah foretold of their coming Messiah in Isaiah 9:6-7,

For unto us a Child is born,
Unto us a Son is given;
And the government will be _____,
And His name will be called
Wonderful, Counselor, _____,
_____, Prince of Peace.
Of the increase of His government and peace
There will be no end,
Upon _____ and over His kingdom,
To order it and establish it with judgment and justice
From that time forward, _____.
The zeal of the LORD of hosts will perform this.

94

Nehemiah prayed this prayer in Nehemiah 1:7–9 while he was held captive in Persia. Nehemiah in his prayer remembered what God had told Moses, "If you are unfaithful, _____ among the Nations." He was fasting and praying to return to Jerusalem.

Lesson 4 Review

Abraham's son Isaac had twins. Which one rejected God?

_____

Jacob had his name changed to _____by God.

How many sons did Jacob have? _____

Which of Jacob's sons was sold as a slave to Egypt and saved his family from famine? _____

Jacob and family moved to Egypt as a group of _____ and four hundred years later they left as a large nation lead by a man named _____.

The Israelites at Mount _____came under the Law.

What was the grievous event this nation committed?

_____

How many years did the Israelites wander the desert? _____

After entering the Promised Land (Canaan), what system of government did they have? _____

Later, they rejected God and wanted a King. Who was the first king? _____

Who was the second king? _____ Third King?

_____

What was the event that divided the kingdom into two?

_____

Both kingdoms, Israel and Judah, went into captivity. Which was the first kingdom to go into captivity?

_____

Notes

Notes

Notes

Lesson 5

WHAT TIME IS IT?

Read Ezra and Nehemiah.

(The books of Daniel, Ezra and Nehemiah were written during and after captivity of the Jews)

In all the countries we lived in for thirteen years, none operated "on time." After arriving on time and sitting alone at the hostess's home, waiting for the party to start, I learned from experience to wait until others arrived. I spent a lot of time sitting in my car outside someone's home, while waiting for other guests to show up. What bothered me more was hosting events and having no one arrive on time!

While living in Mexico, we held a Mexican-style birthday party for our four-year-old daughter, Ashley. Children's birthday parties there meant pulling out all the stops. We hired a clown and a waiter to serve cake and sodas. We set up music outside and hung piñatas.

At starting time, Ashley was dancing around, waiting for her party to begin. But no one was there, not even our international friends. I was panicking. The clown sat on a chair, idly blowing up some balloons. The music guy fiddled with the speakers, glancing at me periodically. My husband wondered when to begin grilling meat.

An hour after the party should have begun, I sat on the bed upstairs fighting tears. Looking out the window, I noticed a few children walking up our driveway. The music started to play, and I saw the clown creating balloon art for our first guests. I rushed out to enjoy the party. In the end, everyone came!

God set a time clock. He is always on time. God didn't keep anyone waiting. The Messiah came after 483 years just as God had told Daniel. The years/weeks prophecy that predicted the Messiah's coming is in Daniel 9:24-27.

After the _____ of Judah's captivity (Jeremiah 29:10), they were allowed to return to the Promised Land/Israel to start rebuilding the wall of the destroyed city of Jerusalem and later the temple. The year that began the return was in 457 B.C. after Artaxerxes issued a _____. (Ezra 7:13) The following next forty-nine years (seven weeks), the Jews rebuilt the city and constructed another temple. The second temple was not as beautiful as the first temple. (Ezra 3:12–13) How did the people feel about the second temple? _____

The Jews returned to an undivided country and the kingdoms of Israel and Judah were one again. They stopped worshipping idols after recognizing the LORD was their one true God. But they were not ruling themselves. They chafed under the rules of foreign countries and desperately wanted their country back, as it had been under King David, and to return to the splendor of King Solomon's reign.

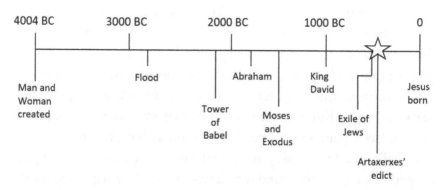

After the 49 years of construction, they waited another 434 years until their Messiah was to come for a total of 483 years. Here is a quick breakdown of the 490 years or 70 weeks into three smaller units:

1. **49 years of construction (seven weeks),** *ALREADY HAPPENED*
2. **434 years (sixty-two weeks)** *ALREADY HAPPENED*
3. **7 years (one week)** *(The Tribulation.)* **STILL TO COME**
   = 490 years (seventy weeks)

If you notice, another way of referring to these 490 years is by "weeks". The Got Questions podcast gives a good explanation of how 70 *"weeks"* is interpreted. Using "weeks" and years makes it a bit harder to understand. The Got Questions says "the angel Gabriel appeared to Daniel and gave him a vision of Israel's future. Gabriel says, in verse 24 of Daniel 9 that seventy weeks are decreed for your people and your holy city. Almost all commentators agree that the seventy "weeks" should be understood as seventy "sevens" of years (7x70=490), in other words, a period of 490 years." So the each "week" should be understood as seven years and then multiply for the total. Keep that in mind as we go through Daniel 9:24-27.

This is an important passage and we'll go through these four verses to help clarify it.

Daniel 9:24-27

"Seventy weeks (490 years) are determined, for your people and for your holy city,
To finish the transgression
To make an end of sins,
To make reconciliation for iniquity,
    (How was the reconciliation made? (2 Corinthians 5:18-19)_____)
To bring in everlasting righteousness,
To seal up vision and prophecy,
And to anoint the Most Holy.

(Who is the Most Holy? (Isaiah 43:3) _____)
Know therefore and understand,
That from the going forth of the command
To restore and build Jerusalem
 (The decree by Artaxerxes in 457 B.C. to rebuild the city (Nehemiah 2:5-8) of Jerusalem kicked off the first seven weeks (49 years).
Until Messiah the Prince,
There shall be seven weeks and sixty-two weeks (total of 483 years or 69 weeks)
 (The Jewish people waited another sixty-two weeks longer (434years), for their Messiah to proclaim Himself as Messiah, which happened on the Triumphal Entry, four days before the crucifixion.)
The street shall be built again, and the wall,
Even in troublesome times.
 (The Jewish people were under the Roman's rule at Jesus' first advent (appearance) and the years were troublesome.)
"And after the sixty-two weeks
Messiah shall be cut off,
 (Jesus put to death on the cross.)
but not for Himself.
 (Here begins the break in the 70-week timeline. After the 483 (7weeks +62weeks x 7) years, the Jewish people rejected their Messiah. The seventieth and final week (or seven years) still is waiting to begin after this 2000-year break called the The Age of Grace or the church age, where we are at the present.

~The rest of the passage is all in the future after the Age of Grace is completed. The coming rapture of the Bride of Christ (Church) will end this age. (1 Thessalonians 4:17, 1 Corinthians 15:51-54)

and the people
 (The "people of the prince" in Daniel 9:26 is thought to be the revived Roman Empire. Read Encyclopedia Britannica's "Treaty of Rome." an international agreement signed on March 25, 1957. Former Roman-conquered countries that signed were Belgium, France, Germany, Italy,

Luxembourg, and the Netherlands and in essence, the revived old Roman Empire. This group later transitioned into the European Union and has added more members.)

of the prince
   (Who is the prince?) _____ *(Ephesians 2:2)*
who is to come
   (The "prince" (not capitalized- does not refer to Christ) is the coming antichrist. He will be ruling during the last week or seven years.)
Shall destroy the city *(Jerusalem)* and the sanctuary *(temple)*.
The end of it shall be with a flood, *(flood of lies, false information)*
And till the end of the war desolations are determined. Then he *(antichrist)* shall confirm a covenant with many for one week; *(seven years)*
But in the middle of the week *(three and half years of the seven)*
He shall bring an end to sacrifice and offering.
And on the wing of abominations
   (an abomination is an event which will shut down the temple sacrificing, possibly sacrificing a pig on the altar as Roman General Titus did in 70 A.D.)
shall be one who makes desolate,
Even until the consummation,
   (All the warfare will consummate (come to a head) at this time when Christ will trodden the nations underfoot (Jeremiah 25:32-33, Revelation 19:11-18)
which is determined,
Is poured out on the desolate."

The last week or seven years is spelled out more completely in the Book of Revelation. It is in the future. It's a time of great suffering and wrath. The antichrist will come to rule the world for seven years. Jesus Christ will defeat the anti-christ at the end of the seven years. (Revelation 19:19-21)
   You may be asking why is there a break in the timeline? Why

wasn't the 70th week completed and why are we still waiting for it? _____We'll cover that in chapter 6.

For Your Information:
Daniel, also interpreted King Nebuchadnezzar's dream of a great image of a man in chapter two of Daniel. This image depicted the four sequential ruling nations listed below and the date they began ruling over the Israelites until the following nation conquered The Promised Land.

1. *The Babylon Empire (head) was made of gold. 612 B.C.*
2. *The Medes/Persians Empire (chest) was made of silver. 549 B.C.*
3. *The Greek Empire (belly) was made of bronze. 336 B.C.*
4. *The Roman Empire (legs and toes) was made of iron and had clay toes. 27 B.C.*

The metal, from gold to iron, demonstrated the strength of each empire's military. Each successive empire got greater and stronger.
The quality of the metal (gold/silver/bronze/iron) demonstrated how efficient each government was. Each successive empire governing process was slower and less efficient. The toes of clay and iron depict the final, future revived Roman Empire, that will rule with the anti-christ during the Tribulation.

The world was now set up for the first advent of Christ. The Roman Empire was in control of the Holy Land as Daniel's "image of the man" (see above) prophecy predicted and the time clock in Daniel, chapter seven, was just about up.

Our Savior was ready to be born and anticipation was high (read Luke 2:25–32). What was Simeon waiting for? _____What did Anna the prophetess look for in Luke 2:36–38? _____

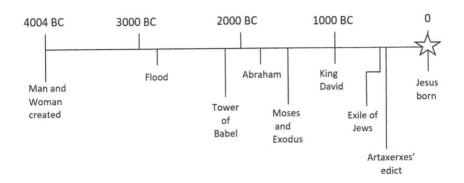

4004 BC	3000 BC	2000 BC	1000 BC	0

Flood

Man and
Woman
created

Tower
of
Babel

Abraham

Moses
and
Exodus

King
David

Exile of
Jews

Artaxerxes'
edict

Jesus
born

DAY 1

A CHILD IS BORN

Read Matthew, Mark, Luke and John

In modern-day Israel, almost all tour buses eventually make their way to Bethlehem. It's a short three-mile journey from Jerusalem. The security is tight. Entering Bethlehem, we traveled through a guarded gate, which was encircled by a barbed-wire-topped wall. These measures have stopped most of the terrorist activity that was prevalent a few years ago. Bethlehem sits in the heart of the conflict between Israel and the Palestinians.

Our tour bus maneuvered around the dusty streets of Bethlehem, arriving at the Church of Nativity. Lines of international tourists flowed out of the church, waiting to see Christ's birthplace marked by a marbled, gold star on the church floor. According to tradition, Christ was born on this location two thousand years ago.

Later we re-boarded our bus and traveled a short distance to the outskirts of Bethlehem to another possible location of Christ's birthplace.

It was a cave, hewn out of rock that was used as a barn. It was suggested that such a cave was used by Mary and Joseph the night Jesus was born and placed in a manger. Our precious LORD, was born in a musty, cramped little stable? Have you wondered why God would choose a stable for the birth of the Savior of the World? The most common explanation I remember given for Christ's stable birth was the humbleness of the location. Did that sound like a hollow explanation to you? It did to me.

I'll present a third option. It doesn't involve the traditional stable. The scripture never used the word "stable", only the word "_____" (Luke 2:12). Where can you find a manger that isn't being used in a stable? There was a location, in the Shepherd's Field, outside Bethlehem. It's called the Migdal Eder or the "_____." (Micah 4:8) Here was a location that included a manger but not in a stable. Priestly shepherds used the high tower to watch for predators of the temple sheep, destined for temple sacrifice.

Inside at the bottom of the tower stood a ceremonially clean manger used as a birthing area for the ewes. Here each newborn lamb was wrapped in swaddling cloths to keep them from flailing and breaking their legs, then placed in the Tower of the Flock manger, inspected for defects and certified, by the priestly shepherds. These certified spotless lambs were to be used for future sacrifice. The shepherds were told by the angels in Luke 2:12, they would find Jesus lying in a manger. The shepherds didn't ask where it was, they knew. And in Luke 2:16, the shepherds found Jesus "lying in a manger." Jesus, the perfect Lamb of God, was then certified for future sacrifice.

Does it make sense that Jesus, our Passover Lamb, at the moment of birth, had to be certified like every sacrificial lamb? _____ (For more information, see *Life and Times of Jesus the Messiah*, by Alfred Eidersheim, and *Mysteries of the Messiah*, by Bill Heinrich.)

Jesus' birth prepared Him for His death.

1. King David was anointed in Bethlehem. The Son of David (Jesus) was born where the line of kings of Judah began.
2. All certified Passover lambs were born in the "Shepherd's Field" by Bethlehem during the second temple period. Jesus was our _____(1 Corinthians 5:7; John 1:29) without _____. (1 Peter 1:19)
3. Where does Micah 5:2 foretell to be the Messiah's birthplace? _____

How would Mary and Joseph find the "Tower of the Flock? After arriving in Bethlehem for the registration for the _____ (Luke 2:2-5), before our Savior was born, they needed a place for Jesus' birth. Luke 2:6 read, "So it was, _____, the days were completed for her to be delivered." Did it appear that they had been in Bethlehem for a bit before Mary went into labor? Would you agree? _____ It was highly possible that they both had relatives there to accommodate their housing needs. After all, they both had originated from King David's royal line of Judah, which had originated from Bethlehem. Possibly for the sake of their relatives they didn't want to give birth at a relatives' home because the people that would come in contact with Mary after labor/birth would have been _____. (Leviticus 15:19)

When Mary's labor began, Joseph searched for a room at the inn, but Bethlehem was bursting at the seams. There were no rooms to be had. God led them to the Migdal Eder (Tower of the Flock), where all the sacrificial lambs were birthed. Jesus said in Matthew 5:17, "Don't think that I came to destroy the law or the prophets. I didn't come to destroy, _____." Jesus' place of birth fulfilled the law in every manner.

What do you think of the Migdal Eder view? Does the scripture support that explanation? _____

Under the law, Mary would have been "unclean" for thirty-three days after the birth of Jesus. Mary and Joseph followed the regulations in Leviticus 12:1-4 and to complete Mary's _____ (Luke 2:22), returned to the temple to offer sacrifice. How do you imagine it was to live under the law? _____

For Further Study

Read the Messianic Psalm 69 for a description of the Jesus' early years before His ministry began.

    *Vs. 8*_____

    Vs. 11-12 _____

DAY 2

EXPECTATIONS

The nation of Israel had come under various covenants that they had made with God. The first covenant was the **Abrahamic Covenant** (lesson 3, day 4), which promised them the following:

- The Promised Land
- A Redeemer and King (Messiah)
- Blessing

They had also agreed to come under the law. (**Mosaic Covenant**) (Lesson 4, day 3). They had a temple and were sacrificing animals, fulfilling the law as God had instructed. Now the Jews expected a Messiah (**Davidic Covenant**) (2 Samuel 7:16) to rule eternally, deliver them, and redeem them from their enemies around them. Zacharias, father of John the Baptist, said in Luke 1:71–77 NKJV, speaking of the Christ-child and what the child would do: "That we should be saved from our _____ and from the hand of all that _____ us; To perform the mercy promised to our fathers, and to _____: The oath which he swore to our father Abraham."

Let's review. At this point, they didn't have control over the deeded Promised Land and were under Roman domination. Daniel's prophecy of sixty-nine weeks (483 years) was nearly up and the kingdom on earth was soon to begin (lesson 5, introduction). They were ready for a change and to cash in on God's promises.

The angel Gabriel told Mary of the child she was to have, "He will be great, and will be called the Son of the Highest: and the Lord God will give Him the _____: And _____; and of His kingdom there will be no end" (Luke 1:32–33). As it had been promised in Zechariah 14:3, their Messiah would _____ for them. They had big expectations.

DAY 3

JESUS DECLARED HE IS GOD AND BEGAN HIS MINISTRY

Before beginning His ministry, John the Baptist, _____ Jesus (Matthew 3:13-15). John the Baptist, Jesus' cousin, was _____, preparing the way before Jesus, mentioned in Malachi 3:1. Jesus then completed forty days of fasting and Satan _____ Him (Mark 1:13).

For Your Information:
Baptism now symbolizes "the _____of regeneration and _____of the Holy Spirit." (Titus 3:5b) We are baptized with the "_____ _____," (John 1:33b) once we put our faith and trust in Jesus.

Jesus began His ministry at _____ years of age (Luke 3:23). He had revealed Himself as _____ (John 4:26) and went about preaching that the _____ was at hand and _____every sickness and every disease. (Matthew 4:17 & 23; 9:35). Jesus also declared to them that He is God. "Most assuredly, I say to you, before Abraham was, _____." (John 8:58; see names of God in the introduction)

I volunteered at a pregnancy help center in Houston. I met some lovely women who were of the Islamic faith. While processing expectant mothers to join our educational program, one of the first

111

things we did was present the gospel using a little booklet called *May I Ask You a Question?* The sweet Muslim ladies always allowed me to go through the little booklet, but at the end of the booklet, each lady would tell me, "I don't believe Jesus was God." I often heard them say, "Jesus was a prophet, a good man," but He was nothing more to them. Muslims do believe that Jesus was one of their prophets and recognize Him as so. That was where I would start to help them know who Jesus is. Muslims count the gospels of Matthew, Mark, Luke, and John as one of their holy books called the Injil. I showed them scriptures in those four books where Jesus declared He is God. Here is a list of those scriptures below.

> Matthew 11:27: _____
> Matthew 28:18: "All authority has been given to me..."
> Luke 5:20, 24: "Man your sins are forgiven you." (Only God can forgive sins).
> Luke 10:22: _____
> John 5:22–23: _____
> John 5:46: "Moses wrote of me" (Deuteronomy 18:17-18).
> John 14:9: _____

Other Scriptures that declare Jesus is God.

> Philippians 2:6
> Colossians 2:9-10
> Titus 2:13
> 2 Peter 1:1

Thinking of Jesus, the Creator of the Universe, how He humbled Himself and became a man that lived as we do is unfathomable. He is fully God and fully man. It said in Philippians 2:8, "And being found in appearance _____, He humbled Himself and became obedient to the point of death, even the death of the cross."

Isaiah 53:3 said, "[Jesus] is despised and rejected by men. A Man of sorrows and acquainted with grief. And we hid, as it were, our faces from Him;_____, and we did not esteem Him." God became a Man, and suffered because of it.

Continuing with His ministry, Jesus arrived in Nazareth, His boyhood town. Jesus went into the synagogue. It was customary on the Sabbath to read a portion of the Torah (Old Testament). Jesus read a familiar portion, Isaiah 61:1–2a. Now think of this: Jesus was reading the prophetic words that were spoken of Him many years ago by Isaiah. The people who were listening were unknowingly watching their Creator, and God, read those prophetic words that Jesus Himself came to fulfill. I can imagine Him unrolling the scroll and finding this passage. And Jesus read:

> "The Spirit of the Lord is upon me, because He has _____to preach the gospel to the poor; He _____ to heal the brokenhearted, to proclaim liberty to the captives, and recovery of sight to the blind, to set at liberty them that are oppressed, To proclaim the acceptable year of the Lord." (Luke 4:18–19)

Jesus closed the book and sat down. Everyone stared at Him. Why were they looking at Him? The reason was that He stopped short of the end of the portion. What He didn't read was "And the day of_____of our God: to comfort all that mourn" (Isaiah 61:2b). The people around Him knew that familiar passage well and knew He had not finished the passage as it customarily was read. Jesus stopped in that exact spot because the rest of the reading dealt with the last week (70th week or last seven years) of the prophecy of Daniel, which would not be fulfilled until later. (Read the chapters of Isaiah 61 through 63 that covered Israel's role in the Tribulation and coming judgment.)

Then Jesus said something shocking. In verse 21 of Luke 4, He said, "Today this scripture _____in your hearing." Jesus was letting them know He is the Messiah, the Anointed One. They wondered and said, "Hey, isn't this Joseph's son?" They weren't convinced.

But now it got really testy. Jesus told them in Luke 4:24b, "No prophet _____in his own country." In Luke 4:25–27, Jesus then pointed out two examples in scripture where Gentiles were used rather than the Jews because of the Jewish rejection of their own prophets. The rejected prophets instead went to Gentiles. The listeners understood that this was a warning. God would go to the Gentiles if the nation of Israel rejected their Messiah.

They were infuriated and were "_____," said in Luke 4:28. They grabbed Jesus and "thrust _____" (Luke 4:29). They led Him to the brow of the hill on which their city was built, that they might throw Him down over the cliff. Not a warm welcome for their Messiah or their fellow citizen of Nazareth. Luke 4:30 said, "Then passing _____them, He went His way." The time for Jesus's death was not at hand, and He left unscathed. It wasn't a joyful hometown reception and He was rejected.

DAY 4

WHO IS THE KINGDOM FOR?

"And the LORD will be King over all the earth." (Zechariah 14:9)

Mark and I flew back home after we had spent one long year overseas in Pakistan. We were anxious to get home, eat an American hamburger, see our family, and relax. We had a layover in Manila, Philippines, for three hours. As we deplaned, a representative of Philippine Air stopped and informed us we had been bumped from our flight and there wasn't another flight for four days. We pleaded with the airline representative, but we no longer had seats on the connecting flight. They had been given away. There was no alternative.

Philippine Airways told us they had a hotel reservation waiting and we could go to the hotel. We reluctantly collected our baggage and then stood in the line to wait for a cab. We waited with many blue-suited business people; taxis would constantly pull up, and the attendant would give the taxi to anyone but us. We were in sweats and blue jeans and felt discriminated against because of our attire. After waiting awhile, we tried to get into any taxi that pulled up because our time to wait had been much longer than anyone around us. Every time we would try to get into a taxi, the attendant would wave us off. We finally sat on our luggage in defeat and gave up. We were at their mercy.

A short while later, a beautiful white stretch limousine glided up in front of our queue. The attendant turned and waved at us to come over. The limo was for us! We were transported to a five-star hotel and spent four days enjoying our complimentary stay. It was like heaven on earth. Why we were selected, I have no idea, but it was wonderful.

The Jews have been selected to gain the kingdom on earth. How wonderful that the King/Messiah came from their people and that one-day, they will rule with the Messiah for eternity. The Jews were waiting for their promised kingdom and the time was very soon, it seemed!

When Jesus began His ministry, He selected twelve disciples and gave them a command in Matthew 10:5-7. It was not a suggestion but a command. "These twelve Jesus sent out and commanded them saying, "_____ go into the way of the Gentiles, and _____. But go rather to the lost sheep of the house of _____. And as you go, preach, saying, "The kingdom of heaven is at hand."

Let's look at this command a little closer. First, He said do *not* go to the Gentiles or the Samaritans. The kingdom was being offered to the Jews—and *no one else*. Read Matthew 15:21–28, it revealed more details to whom Jesus made the offer of the kingdom and how firm that command was. In that passage, a Canaanite (Gentile) woman called out to Jesus and she recognized who He was. She said, "Have mercy on me. O Lord, Son of David! My daughter is severely demon-possessed."

Jesus ignored her. The scripture said, "But He answered her not a word." The disciples, in verse 23, urged Jesus to send her away. (The disciples were not being mean but simply following Jesus's command to go only to Israel.)

In verse 24, Jesus answered her, "I was not sent except to the lost sheep of the _____."

The Canaanite woman pleaded and said, "Lord, help me."

Jesus refused again. He said, "It is not good to take the children's (Jews) bread and throw it to the little dogs." (Gentiles were often referred to as dogs in that era.) And then came the most amazing response from this lady. Her understanding was far beyond all of the Jews around Jesus.

She said, "Yes Lord yet even the little dogs eat the crumbs which fall from their masters' table". She knew who He was, her Master and Creator.

Then Jesus answered and said to her, "O woman, great is your faith! Let it be to you as you desire." And her daughter was healed from that very hour.

How could she have gained such an understanding of who Jesus was? _____

What Is a "Table"?

A "table" is what is offered to you. Jesus was offering a "table" to the Jews. The Canaanite woman understood that and used the same reference in above story when she used "Master's table". The word table is often used in meetings as issues are "tabled" for the next meeting. It waits for us to take it or leave it, decision-wise. Psalm 69:22 says, "Let their table become a snare before them: and their well-being a trap." Paul used the same verse in Romans 11:9–10, referring to the Jews. The "table" was the offer of the King and the kingdom to the descendants of Abraham. Did they take it or leave it? _____

Another instance of Jesus not dealing with Gentiles was right before the crucifixion. Jesus was told there were Greeks who wanted to see Him in John 12:20–26. Jesus refused to see them and said in verse 24, "The hour has come that the Son of Man should be glorified. Most assuredly, I say to you, unless a grain of wheat falls into the ground and _____, it remains alone; but if it dies, it produces much grain." Jesus was explaining that He had to die first, for the Gentiles to be included. It wasn't time, yet.

The kingdom was only being offered to the Jewish people. (The rejection of their Messiah will bring in the Age of Grace. We will cover that in lesson 7.)

What will the kingdom be like? Read Isaiah 11:6–10 and Isaiah 2:1–4. Write a description of the millennial kingdom.

_____.

The twelve disciples had "kingdom fever" as well. In Matthew 19:27–29, the question they asked Jesus was "See, we have_____, and followed You; therefore _____?" They were asking, what do we get, what is our reward for their faithfulness? Do you think that was proper? _____

Jesus answered them and said in verse 28, "Assuredly I say to you, that in the regeneration (millennial kingdom), when the Son of Man _____, you who have followed Me will also _____ judging the twelve tribes of Israel." That must have been great to hear! They would rule over Israel in the kingdom!

Being rewarded is a part of life. I can't say I blame those twelve disciples asking what they would receive for following Jesus. When I was about seven years old, I inherited a job from my older sister. She sold greeting cards and the sales brought in a bit of money. She would take our little red wagon loaded with cards and go up and down our hilly town, knocking at doors. By the time we younger sisters got assigned the job, my mother was in full charge of the business. My oldest sister was gone at college, and we pulled that wagon all over town. What my mom forgot to do was reward our efforts. Not receiving profits from our efforts made it a tedious chore, and we had zero enthusiasm and sold very little. I think the disciples were motivated the same way. The reward was very helpful.

The disciples were selected to help Jesus and to spread the news that the Kingdom was at hand. Jesus performed the following signs and miracles during His earthly three-year ministry to prove to Israel that He was their Messiah-King, the God whom their fathers worshipped. The following seven signs are from the Gospel of John and summarized Jesus' ministry. (There are not enough pages in any book to write all Jesus did on earth.)

1. John 2:1-11---Changed water into wine
2. John 4:46-54---Healed Official's son
3. John 5:1-18---Healed lame man at the pool by the Sheep Gate
4. John 6:1-14---Fed the five thousand
5. John 6:16-21---Walked on the sea
6. John 9:1-41---Sight restored
7. John 11:1-44---Raised Lazarus from the dead

The Jews had always required a sign. Jesus speaking to the Jews said in John 4:48. "Unless you people see _____, you will by no means believe." The Jewish requirement of signs began during the exodus from Egypt under Moses' leading. God gave Moses three signs to perform for the people. Exodus 4:30-31 told us that after the signs were given, then the people believed. Here are other requests for signs asked from Jesus during His ministry. (Luke 11:16, Matthew 24:3, Matthew 16:1-4.) In 1 Corinthians 1:22, Paul said, "For Jews request _____and the Greeks seek after _____."

After three years of signs and miracles during His ministry, that proved He is God and also the Messiah, it was now time to proclaim His Messiah ship. Let's move onto the Tenth of Nissan on Day 5.

DAY 5

THE TRIUMPHAL ENTRY

The Tenth of Nissan

On _____ of Nissan (first month of the year) (Exodus 12:3) every Jewish family chose a Passover lamb for sacrifice on the _____ of Nissan (Exodus 12:6) Passover Day. This was an annual event since God in Egypt gave this ordinance over one thousand five hundred years earlier. Passover was to be a _____. (Exodus 12:14a). (See Lesson 4)

After the construction of the temple and many years after the first Passover, the custom began that the high priest would choose a national Passover lamb to be sacrificed as a nation. Tradition tells us that the high priest selected a perfect, spotless lamb born in the Shepherd's Field by Bethlehem. And probably on the morning of the tenth of Nissan, high priest Caiaphas exited through the Damascus gate on a donkey on the north side of the city, to fetch a lamb from the hills around Bethlehem.

Within the city of Jerusalem, the crowds of pilgrims gathered and waited in anticipation of the arrival of the national Passover lamb, with palm fronds in their hands. Scores of priests lined the city streets and waited for Caiaphas's return with the lamb on his lap.

While Caiaphas was out collecting the national Passover lamb, Jesus entered the Eastern Gate on a donkey. Jesus didn't need a lamb on His lap; He *is* the spotless Lamb and at the same time, a

Priest of the Order of Melchizedek. The waiting pilgrims started to shout, "Hosanna (to save, rescue, savior) to the _____! Blessed is He who comes in the name of the LORD Hosanna in the highest" and laid down their palm fronds in front of Jesus (Matthew 21:8-9). The Pharisees, anxiously waiting for the High Priest Caiaphas and his lamb, said unto Jesus in Luke 19:39, "Teacher, _____ Your disciples." Jesus replied, "I tell you that, if these should keep silent, _____ would immediately cry out" (verse 40). Jesus continued on His way to the temple.

For your Information: Why did the triumphal entry crowd use palm leaves, spread cloaks and shout the words they said?

The pilgrims shouted the words, "Blessed is he who comes in the name of the LORD! We have blessed you from the house of the LORD." Those words come from Psalm 118:26, a Messianic Psalm that would be often sung by a procession on their way to the temple.

Spreading of their cloaks on the ground was the sign of royalty for their king. (2 Kings 9:13)

Why palm branches? (Leviticus 23:40 and Revelation 7:9) A Palm branch was a sign of victory.

Why did Jesus ride on a donkey? He fulfilled the prophecy of Zechariah 9:9. Write the verse here. _____ Riding on a donkey meant you came in peace. Contrast it to the _____ horse Jesus will ride in Revelation 19:11-16. Coming on a horse means war and judgment.

Soon after Jesus' Triumphal entry, high priest Caiaphas arrived with the national Passover lamb on his lap. The crowds had dispersed and had already shouted their "hosannas" for their Lamb, the Holy One of Israel.

Through this act, Jesus had declared Himself the Messiah and Caiaphas was not in agreement with it.

For More Information: Biblesearchers.com has a detailed article titled "Jesus as the Passover Lamb."

This stoked the fire to set the Caiaphas into action to do away with Jesus. Later on, Caiaphas and his fellow priests, scribes, and elders got together to make a plan "to take Jesus by _____, and kill Him" (Matthew 26: 3–5). Caiaphas continued on his un-hailed journey and delivered the national Passover lamb to the temple with little fanfare. The little lamb would be on display for everyone to inspect, designated for slaughter on Nissan 14, at 3:00 p.m.

Our Israel tour in 2014 included seeing the Eastern Gate in Jerusalem that Jesus entered on the 10th of Nissan. The gate is located on the only surviving part of the wall that surrounded the former temple mount.

Fun Fact

Jesus' Triumphal Entry came on the Year of the Jubilee, which occurred every fifty years. It was a year for all debts and bondage to be released and forgiven (Leviticus 25:9-10, 23–55). All tribal lands were returned to the original owners. Jesus proclaimed this coming event in Luke 4:19. "To proclaim the *acceptable year of the LORD.*" It was another name for the *Jubilee Year.* The Jubilee year presented a beautiful picture of the New Testament theme of redemption and forgiveness. Christ the Redeemer came to set us free as slaves and prisoners of sin.

The Sultan Suleiman sealed up the Eastern Gate in 1541 A.D.; no one has walked through that gate since medieval times. He sealed the gate to prevent the Jewish Messiah from entering the Eastern Gate of Jerusalem, as it is prophesied in Ezekiel 44:1–3. The gate faces the Garden of Olives, with the Kidron Valley centered between the two locations.

After we toured the former temple mount, our tour group went down the Kidron Valley and then walked up to the Mount of Olives, where we had a good view of the beautiful Eastern Gate. It's sealed for now, but that won't stop Jesus from one day from entering by that gate!

Lesson 5 Review

Who prophesied that 483 years would pass before the Messiah would appear? (He was a captive in Babylon) _____
Who decreed the Jews could return to Jerusalem (and started the time clock) to begin building the wall and temple in 457 B.C.?

_____

Did Israel have a king after captivity?

_____

Where was Jesus born and David anointed as king?

_____

What are three covenants made with Israel by God? _____
Jesus' ministry, in part, was to provide signs that he was Israel's Messiah. T or F

Notes

Notes

Notes

Lesson 6

JESUS THE MESSIAH REJECTED BY HIS PEOPLE

"And the light shines in the darkness, and the darkness
did not comprehend it."
—John 1:5

Mark and I had been married for six months in January of 1986, and
he was working in Henan Province, deep in the heart of China. He
worked a rotation that consisted of two months in China and two
months off in the United States. He asked me to accompany him for
his last two-month rotation and we traveled together to the middle
of China. China had just opened its doors to the west after Mao
Zedong's death in 1976, but it still had little outside influence. No
one spoke a word of English.

When I de-boarded the plane in Beijing, we got onto an old
steam engine train that looked like it was straight out of an old
Western movie. The ancient train belched out smoke and steam and
transported us on an eight-hour bumpy journey in a sleeper car to
central China. We spoke no Mandarin, and every sign we tried to
read was in Chinese characters.

Arriving at the Henan train depot, we were met by our translator,
named Weng. Weng had been educated in the United Kingdom
and had a pronounced British-Chinese accent. I was a very green

Midwestern girl who had never been out of the Midwest. I was accustomed to a Midwestern American accent, and when Weng began speaking his super-fast accented Queen's English, I didn't understand a word he uttered.

Weng, Mark, and I spent two months riding together in a car during my stay. At the end of those two months, I still didn't understand a word Weng said. Mark had become our interpreter because he had no problems understanding Weng. I thought I would eventually start to pick up on Weng's accent and begin to understand but that didn't happen. He spoke perfect English, excellent grammar, and yet, I couldn't communicate with him. Weng often exclaimed to Mark, "Why can't she understand me?" I felt terrible.

Jesus too, spoke with His fellow countrymen and they didn't understand His message. But they had a different problem. When He spoke, His words were understood, but it was a heart problem. He ministered for three years and yet very few of them understood that He was their King/Messiah. He spoke their language, and understood their customs, but they were completely in the dark. In 1 Corinthians 2:8, it said, "which none of the rulers of this age knew; for had they known, they would not _____."

Israel didn't know and understand that the King of Glory was talking and living with them. Our next five days of Lesson Six portrays the final days of Jesus's life before His death and resurrection. Every event that occurred had significance while Jesus was fulfilling every point of the law. This is the culmination of why Jesus had become a man and was now ready to die. God did everything legally as He redeemed mankind through His Son.

From the day Adam sinned, God had promised a coming Redeemer. Let's go through Passover week day by day to see how that promise was fulfilled through Jesus our Savior.

DAY 1

JESUS FULFILLED THE PASSOVER

The Tenth of Nissan: Saturday

Let's return to the tenth of Nissan, the day of the Triumphal Entry. Jesus went to the temple after His Triumphal Entry. He cleansed it at the beginning of His ministry (John 2:15–16), and now He cleansed it again.

The second temple cleansing was in Matthew 21:12–17. Verse twelve said, "Then Jesus went into the temple of God and drove out _____". After the cleansing, Jesus stayed and verse 14 said, "_____ and He healed them". The chief priests and scribes watched the wonderful things He did and were indignant. At the same time, children were shouting in the temple, "_____" (Matthew 21:15). Jesus left the temple that evening and spent the night at Bethany.

For Your Information:
Alfred Edersheim wrote in "The Life and Times of Jesus the Messiah" that both Josephus (historian in the first century) and rabbinic writings stated that Annas, the father-in-law of Caiaphas the high priest, and Caiaphas were in charge of the "Temple-market." They were making a big profit of overcharging people coming to Jerusalem for the Passover and other festivals.

Let's compare Jesus, the Lamb of God and the national Passover lamb that High Priest Caiaphas brought from the Bethlehem hills. They each paralleled the other until the fourteenth of Nissan. Jesus was at the temple for people to question and ascertain that He was their Messiah. They looked for faults. At the same time, the national Passover lamb was on display for people to check the lamb for imperfections.

The Eleventh of Nissan: Sunday

Jesus returned to the temple the next morning. The chief priest and elders confronted Him again looking for faults (Matthew 21:23–46). Later on, the Pharisees, Scribes, and Sadducees tried to trip Him up with some tricky questions. They didn't succeed. Why do you think Jesus spoke to the Pharisees, priests, Sadducees, and scribes in parables in Matthew chapters 22 and 23?

_____

The Twelfth of Nissan: Monday

On this day, Mary anointed Jesus with an expensive ointment in Bethany (Matthew 26:6–12). Jesus explained why she had anointed Him in verse 12. What was the reason? _____

On this same day, Judas looked into the betrayal of Jesus. Read Matthew 26:14–16. How many pieces of silver did the chief priests pay Judas for his coming betrayal of Christ? _____

The Thirteenth of Nissan: Tuesday

The disciples and Jesus ate the Lord's Supper together in Matthew 26:17–29. _____ departed to betray Jesus (John 13:30) during the meal. The Lord's Supper was on the thirteenth and fourteenth of Nissan as the evening closed in. They left the meal after the new day began after 6:00 pm.

The Fourteenth of Nissan:
Wednesday, after 6:00 p.m. (Late Evening)

Jesus and the disciples (minus Judas) left after the Lord's Supper to go to the garden of Gethsemane to _____ (Matthew 26:36).

Later, after Jesus prayed, _____ arrived at the garden and was accompanied by a great multitude with swords and _____ (Matthew 26:47). *Jesus was arrested* (Matthew 26:47–56). The disciples fled. Jesus was led away to Caiaphas the high priest, and others who were assembled. What other groups were awaiting Jesus to condemn Him? _____ (Matthew 26:57)

This began a long, lonely, excruciating day for Jesus. We'll pick up with the continuation of the fourteenth of Nissan, Crucifixion Day, on day 2.

DAY 2

JESUS IS CONDEMNED

Fourteenth of Nissan: Wednesday (Sunset to Sunset) _Passover Day_

This was a very action-packed night. From the garden of Gethsemane, where Jesus was arrested, Jesus was taken to the Sanhedrin in the middle of the night. (The Sanhedrin was a council of seventy-one Jewish elders and scribes headed by Caiaphas, the high priest.) The Sanhedrin had religious, civil, and criminal jurisdiction for their own people, the Jews. While questioning Jesus, Caiaphas tore his clothes. What did Jesus say that provoked Caiaphas to tear his clothes? _____ (Matthew 26:64-65) According to the high priest regulations that were given in Leviticus 21:10, the high priest was never to tear his clothes and this symbolically ended Caiaphas' priesthood. (Keep in mind, Jesus is a Priest by order of _____ and fulfilled those duties as well in the heavenly tabernacle. (Hebrews 5:6; Hebrews 7:1-3))

During the night, the Sanhedrin condemned Jesus to death. What words were said to condemn Jesus in Matthew 26:66? _____ As morning dawned, they bound Jesus and led Him to _____, the governor. (Matthew 27:2; John 18:28)

Caiaphas had scurried off to the temple to fulfill his high priestly duties on a very busy Passover day. The temple priests were in full

132

production of preparing for the thousands of sacrificial lambs brought by the pilgrims, to shed their blood across the altar before 3:00 pm.

Jesus was taken to Pilate because the Jews were not allowed by the Romans to crucify their own people. Only stoning was allowed for the Jews to mete out. Caiaphas and his henchmen wanted to give Jesus the worst death possible and that would be crucifixion. Caiaphas and company had to involve the Romans to secure a crucifixion death for Jesus. (Notice both Jews and Gentiles were complicit in Christ's death.)

Pilate tried to get out of condemning Jesus to death. He even sent Jesus to _____. (Luke 23:6-11) But what was the crowd shouting? _____ (Luke 23:20-22) Pilate succumbed to the pressure. But before he did, he stated, "I find no fault with this man." Pilate said it in concert with Caiaphas, the high priest, at the temple, who had the national Passover lamb in his arms and declared, "I find no fault with this lamb." Both lambs were perfect.

After declaring the national lamb perfect at the temple, it was led to the slaughtering area to die. Jesus, the perfect Passover Lamb was led to _____ to die (Matthew 27:31-33). Both Lambs, the Lamb of God and the national Passover lamb were _____ (Matthew 26:63; Isaiah 53:7). The wooden crossbar was thrown across Jesus's shoulders just like Isaac carried the wood for the sacrifice, two thousand years ago (John 19:17) (See lesson 3, day 5, chart for comparison of Christ's sacrifice to Isaac's near sacrifice).

The national Passover lamb at the temple was bound for slaughter. Jesus was crucified (bound and nailed on the cross) at Golgotha. It was closing in on the ninth hour (3:00 p.m.). Right before 3:00 p.m., high priest Caiaphas at the temple turned to the surrounding priests and said, "I thirst," in concert with Jesus, High Priest from the order of Melchizadek, suffering on the cross, called to the guards, stating, " _____."(John 19:28) Jesus was offered a _____ (John 19:29) with vinegar. (A hyssop was used to paint on the blood to the doorposts during the First Passover in Egypt; Exodus 12:22-23)

Caiaphas raised his hand and with the knife, killed the temple lamb, and cried out, "It is finished," in concert with Jesus, also High Priest/Lamb, the King of Glory, who cried, "_____". Jesus, who was both Lamb and Priest, "gave up _____". (John 19:30)

At that moment, the earth started shaking and rumbling. The sky was dark and the veil in the temple was "torn _____" in the Holy of Holies (Matthew 27:51). The centurion who watched the crucifixion summed it up best in Matthew 27:54 "_____." *The Creator had been murdered by His creation.* What was the significance of the three-inch thick veil in the temple being torn from top to bottom? Exodus 26:33 will help explain it. _____

Jesus died at 3:00 p.m. This was a problem for the law-abiding Jews. The fourteenth of Nissan was a preparation day that preceded the *High Sabbath* on the fifteenth of Nissan. The fifteenth of Nissan was a High Sabbath day or a holiday, and it began in three hours. They had to get Jesus off of the cross and bury Him in the tomb before 6:00 p.m. (Under the law, you can't work on the Sabbath; Mark 15:42.) Also, Deuteronomy 21:22–23 commanded that if someone was put to death by hanging on a tree, you couldn't let his body remain _____ upon the tree. They had two reasons to quickly take Him off of the cross.

How do you imagine they felt as they rushed and carried Jesus' body and placed Him in the tomb? _____

What is a High Sabbath Day?

John 19:31 said, "The Jews therefore, because it was the _____, that the bodies should not remain upon the cross on the Sabbath day (for that Sabbath day was a _____)." The high Sabbath was the fifteenth day of Nissan, First Day of the Feast of Unleavened Bread. It was one of the seven *high Sabbath days*. Numbers 28:17–18 stated, "You shall do no _____" on the fifteenth of Nissan. This High Sabbath/holiday fell on a Thursday that year. (Leviticus chapter 23 has a list of all seven High Sabbaths feasts and the calendar days they were observed yearly.)

The point being made is that the crucifixion was not necessarily on Friday, as we traditionally observe it. A High Sabbath can fall on any day of the week, similar to Christmas, December 25, which also falls on any day of the week.

DAY 3

JESUS IN THE TOMB

This is the first year I didn't post a sibling picture on Facebook or Instagram on "sibling day." It was too painful. We lost our big sister. When growing up, we were called "the five Johnson girls." We had many photos of all five of us in the past, but we will not be able to take any more in the future. Joette passed away of a raging infection, very unexpectedly, on August 5, 2019. When I received that heartbreaking early-morning phone call, a beautiful sunrise was occurring out our big windows. I thought of her flying over us, heading home to be with her Savior.

My sister, Melody, was visiting, and after receiving the news, I slipped into bed with her, just as we used to sleep in one bed when we were little girls. She slept on a blow-up mattress in front of our large windows, facing east. We watched that glorious sunrise together but felt extremely broken and forlorn. We will miss her.

That is how I imagine the disciples and the women that watched Jesus die the evening before felt on that empty painful morning after the crucifixion. Some had some huge regrets. Peter had denied Him. The others had run away. I'm sure they all felt they could have done better. They undoubtedly wished they could have changed the outcome.

The next few days were feast days for the Jews. Those following feast days must have been observed with very little joy for the followers of Jesus. Let's detail what occurred each day Jesus was in the tomb. (See summary in *"What is a High Sabbath Day?"*)

The Fifteenth of Nissan (6:00 p.m.–6:00 p.m.), High Sabbath Day- Thursday

- Jesus's first day in the tomb.
- All the Jewish people were eating their Passover meal. They had to eat it all by _____, as commanded in Exodus 12:10.
- The fifteenth of Nissan was the first day (seven days in total) of the- **Feast of the Unleavened Bread.**

The Feast of the Unleavened Bread was celebrated by cleaning out the yeast in all Jewish homes. They swept and cleaned every bit out. What did this have to do with Christ's sacrifice on the cross? Paul explained it best in 1 Corinthians 5:7–8 NKJV, which said, "Therefore purge out the _____, that you may be a new lump, since you truly are unleavened. For indeed Christ, _____, was sacrificed for us."

Leaven represented sin, and what better festival to have the day after Christ paid the debt of sin? This day of celebration that fell the day following Jesus's crucifixion wasn't a coincidence. When John the Baptist saw Jesus the first time, he exclaimed, "Behold the Lamb of God who _____!" (John 1:29) John the Baptist knew whom Jesus was and what He was being sent to accomplish.

This festival represented this new and wonderful state of the world after the crucifixion. The effects of sin haven't been lifted as of yet, but it has been paid for by Christ's sacrifice. Hebrews 10: 12–14 says, "But this Man, after He had offered _____sacrifice for sins forever, sat down at the right hand of God, from that time _____are made His footstool. For by one offering He has _____ those who are being sanctified."

When will the effects of sin be lifted? (Revelation
21:1-5.) _____

Sixteenth of Nissan: Friday

- Jesus's second day in the tomb
- Another preparation day before a regular weekday Sabbath.
- Luke 23:55-56 told that the women went to the tomb, observed
  His body, and then they went to prepare _____
  to later anoint Jesus' body. The women would return to anoint
  Jesus on Sunday morning, because they _____ on the
  Sabbath/Saturday.
- The chief priests and the Pharisees gathered together in
  front of Pilate. They feared the disciples would come and
  _____ and claim that Christ had risen from
  the dead on the third day (Matthew 27:63–66). Pilate agreed
  to help and set a watch of soldiers.

Seventeenth of Nissan: Saturday (Weekly Sabbath Day of Rest)

- All Jews were at home observing the Sabbath.
- Jesus' third day in the tomb.

Where was Jesus' spirit during the three days His body was in the
tomb?

Read the following scriptures and write where you find the location.

Ephesians 4:9 _____
Acts 2:31 _____

Where was Hell/Hades/Sheol understood to be located in the Old
Testament?

Numbers 16:30–34 _____

Isaiah 14:9-11 _____

Ezekiel 31:16-18 _____

Ezekiel 32:18-21 _____

Jesus told us where He would be after the crucifixion in Matthew 12:40. Jesus said, "The Son of Man be three days and three nights in the _____." Why would Jesus' Spirit descend into Hell during the three days of His body in the tomb? _____

In Luke 16:22–26, Jesus explained Hell/Hades and Paradise further by the story of the rich man and Lazarus. The rich man was in Hades, but he could see Lazarus in Abraham's bosom or Paradise. This passage said there is a "great gulf fixed" or separation between Hades and Paradise. Paradise was on the other side of Hell. Also while on the cross, Jesus told the believing thief "today you will be with Me _____." (Luke 23:43b) Why were believers located in Paradise and not heaven at this point? _____

The reason was that the ransom/debt had to be paid first for our sin. Jesus accomplished payment with His sinless, sacrificial blood on the cross. Only until the debt was cancelled could the captives/ransomed go to a sinless Heaven. The believers that had waited in Paradise were then set free. Jesus said in Mark 10:45, "For even the Son of Man did not come to be served but to serve and to give His life as a _____ for many." The ransomed were being held captive by sin.

In Ephesians 4:8, Paul quoted Psalm 68:18 (speaking of Jesus), which said, "When He ascended on high, He _____ captivity captive". The ransomed or captive were led to heaven after the ransom was paid at the cross. In Psalm 49:15, the Psalmist knew this and said, "But God will redeem my soul from the power _____, for He will receive me." The psalmist was waiting in Paradise for Jesus to come and lead him and the other believers to heaven.

Review Luke 4:18, where Jesus, in His hometown of Nazareth, read the Isaiah 61:1 passage. Part of the passage said, "To proclaim liberty to the captives," which He proclaimed when He descended into Paradise at his death in the period between His death and resurrection. King David in Psalm 16:10 said, "For You _____ Sheol (Paradise side of Hell), nor will You allow Your Holy One to see corruption." King David was freed as well.

What are your thoughts on the above paragraphs? _____ Where do believers go <u>now</u> after Jesus' payment on the cross? Paul told us in 2 Corinthians 5:8 that "to be _____ from the body and to be present with the Lord". We will be in heaven with our Lord at the moment our bodies die. Jesus is in heaven and we join him after our bodies die.

DAY 4

RESURRECTION DAY

Eighteenth of Nissan: Sunday

- When did the women return to the tomb to anoint Jesus' body and discover the empty tomb? _____ (Mark 16:2; John 20:1). After reading the above scripture, when did Jesus rise from the dead, Saturday or Sunday? _____
- Sunday was the first day of the **Feast of the First Fruits.**
- **The Empty Tomb Is Discovered.** In Matthew 28:6: the angel proclaims, "He is not here: _____, as He said. Come, see the place where the Lord lay." (Matthew 28:1–8; Mark 16:2–8; Luke 24:1–7; John 20:1-18)

To ponder: Do you agree with this timeline?

_____

Why weren't the disciples waiting at the tomb for the Lord to rise Sunday morning? Here are some of the scriptures where they were told Jesus would rise again on the third day.

Matthew 16:21 _____

Matthew 20:17-19 _____

Luke 9:22b _____

Luke 24:7-8 _____

Luke 18:34 told us that "they (disciples) understood none of these things; this saying was _____ from them, and they _____ the things which were spoken." Why do you think it was hidden from them? _____

Arriving in Venezuela in 1988, we didn't speak a word of Spanish. We found a favorite restaurant that we frequented our first few months of living there, but because of the language barrier, we basically nodded and smiled at the host and the wait staff. The restaurant employees were always very friendly but formal, because we couldn't hold much of a conversation.

We left for our summer break to the USA and a few months later returned to Venezuela. After our arrival, we returned to our favorite restaurant. When we entered the door, everyone gasped and stared at us for a good twenty seconds. The host dashed over and gave Mark and me a huge hug. The rest of the wait staff joined for a group hug. We were completely confused at their reaction to seeing us. They were excitedly speaking all at once, and with our rudimentary Spanish, it was hard to understand. We finally got it sorted out. They had heard that Mark and I had gotten into a horrible car accident up the road early in the summer and didn't survive. For them, the first time seeing us again was like we had come back to life.

Begotten Son

What does "begotten" mean? John 3:16a says, "For God so loved the world that He gave His only Begotten Son." Read the context around this verse, especially verse 14. Is the scripture speaking of Jesus's death or birth? _____Acts 13:30–34 explained what "begotten" meant. What does begotten refer to? _____
Read the supporting references: Hebrews. 5:5; Hebrews 1:5; Revelation 1:5; Colossians 1:15–18; 1 Peter 1:3; Psalm 2:7.

Jesus is the only *Begotten* Son <u>from the dead</u>. He still has His sinless body He used on earth in heaven. Jesus displayed His _____on His body after His Crucifixion. (John 20:20, Zechariah 13:6) Jesus didn't see _____(Acts 13:35; Psalm 16:10). We, as sinful beings, will need new, uncorrupted bodies in eternity.

The sight of Jesus that early Sunday morning was a wonderful and yet a world-shaking moment. The last time the women had seen Jesus, He was on the cross, bruised and severely beaten and barely recognizable. Now a resurrected Jesus was with them again. It would have been hard to compute. What had happened? They must have been shaking with joy and wonder in the cool morning light. Maybe they rubbed their eyes in amazement. *He's alive!* But Jesus also told Mary not to touch Him.

Jesus told her (John 20:15–18), "Do not _____ to Me, _____;" Then a short time later, He saw other people and encouraged them to touch Him (John 20:27; Luke 24:39). Why couldn't Mary touch Jesus at that moment?

Hebrews 8 and 9 will help explain it. Jesus was the Passover Lamb, but He also was a High Priest of the order of Melchizedek (Hebrews 7:17). Jesus still had His priestly duties to perform. Jesus said He must "ascend to the Father" because Jesus had to go to the perfect tabernacle (Hebrews 8:2) in heaven, made without hands, to offer the **First Fruits** sheaf offering that was instituted by God in Leviticus 23:10-12. Jesus our High Priest was sanctified, ready to make the first fruits sacrifice after His resurrection. It said in 1 Corinthians 15:20 "But now Christ is risen from the dead, and has become the firstfruits of those who have fallen asleep." Mary couldn't touch Him at that point before He fulfilled His priestly duties.

For Your Information:
*The **Feast of the First Fruits** shows the orderly three-stage process of the Resurrection. First Corinthians 15:23 says "But every man in his own order: Christ the _____; afterward they that are Christ's at His coming." Jesus' resurrection began the harvest of the resurrection.*

1. *The first part of the feast began with the omer or sheaf of grain, which was offered by the priest called a wave offering. The farmer would pick the first ripening stalks of grain, made a sheaf and then brought it to the priest to be offered.*

   Jesus was the first resurrected person. Matthew 27:52-53 said, the "bodies in the grave came out _____ his resurrection." The sheaf was completed by these resurrected souls and this sheaf was offered by Jesus as High Priest, resurrection morning, when He ascended to His Father.

2. *The second part of the harvest was when the field was fully ripened, the farmer would harvest it all at one time. That refers to the coming rapture, when Christ's Bride/Church will be brought to heaven all at once, along with the "dead in Christ" in the grave (bodies only because their souls are in heaven). And the dead in Christ will rise _____. Then we _____ and remain shall _____ with them in the clouds to meet the Lord in the air." (1 Thessalonians 4:16b-17a) One day in the future the entire Church or Bride of Christ will leave together in a _____ at the last trumpet (1 Corinthians 15:50-52).*

3. *The final part of the harvest is the corners of the field. The corners are left un-harvested to be harvested later on (in Bible times, left for the poor. (Leviticus 23:22) You might remember the story of Ruth and Boaz in Ruth 2:8-9. Ruth gleaned the un-harvested corners of Boaz's fields.) Those corners represent the people who will come to know Christ during the Tribulation and Millennium.*

My parents visited us in Pakistan in 1988. I took a little time off from teaching and we went up a small mountainous village outside of Gilgit, Pakistan. It was a beautiful, untouched region in the Karakoram Mountain Range. We stayed a few days and took a few jeep trips around the area. But our favorite part was sitting outside our hotel. Our rustic hotel was built into a grassy hill, and there were flowers and butterflies along with the crisp, clean mountain air. A grizzled shepherd would come daily with his little flock of sheep and let them graze on the emerald grass in front of our hotel. We would take our afternoon tea on lawn chairs outside our rooms and watch those little lambs frolic, dance and chase each other in late afternoon sunset. It was wonderful entertainment.

I think of the thousands of lambs during the Israel's temple period that were sacrificed and their blood was shed. I'm sure they were as darling as the innocent lambs we saw in the Karakoram Mountains. Have you wondered why their blood was needed?

The reason blood was needed for sacrifices was explained in Leviticus 17:11 it said "_____ is in the blood, and I have given it to you upon the _____ to make _____ for your souls; for it is the _____ that makes atonement for the soul." In the New Testament after Christ's shedding of His blood on the cross, the Bible explained it further in the book of Hebrews. Hebrews 9:22 stated that "And according to the law almost all things are _____ with blood, without the shedding of _____, there is no remission." Also Ephesians 1:7 said "In Him we have _____ through His blood." Along with Romans 5:9a, which said, "having now been _____by his blood." We need no more sacrifices because Jesus provided His sinless, perfect blood that justified and provided redemption for us when we put our faith and trust in Jesus. Those little lambs no longer are needed.

Will we have blood in our bodies in eternity? After the crucifixion Jesus appeared to many. He said in Luke 24:39, "Behold My hands and My feet, that it is I Myself. Handle me and see for a spirit does not _____, as you see me have." Notice Jesus mentioned flesh and bones, but not blood. Paul said in Philippians 3:21a that Jesus will "transform our lowly body that it may be conformed to His glorious body," Could that possibly mean we will not have blood in eternity, only bones and flesh? What do you think? _____ We know we will have new, glorious bodies!

DAY 5

PREPARING FOR THE KINGDOM!

Read Acts.

Living in a foreign country took a lot of preparation and planning for before an impending move. We would do a "big shop" of items not found in the country we were relocating. Spices, marshmallows, cans of cranberries, chocolate chips, and clothing were some of the items we packed. We brought contact solution, medicines, and comfort items such as magazines, books, and cosmetics. Thinking through all the lists of items was an overwhelming task. We knew it was worth it because with good planning, it made the transition much easier.

The disciples were thinking about the kingdom and the changes that it would bring for them and Israel. Their mindset was evident. At the moment before Jesus ascended to heaven, the very last question asked by the disciples was in Acts 1:6: "Lord, will You at this time _____ kingdom to Israel?" The disciples were looking forward to ruling under Jesus on the twelve thrones over the twelve tribes of Israel. Let's get this kingdom started!

Jesus answered them: "It is not for you to _____ which the Father has put in His own authority. But you shall receive power when the Holy Spirit has come upon you; and you shall be witnesses to Me in Jerusalem, and in all Judea and Samaria, and to the end of the earth" (Acts 1:7–8).

Jesus doesn't answer directly about the timing of the Millennium, when He will set up His kingdom and rules on Earth. He told the disciples that it's not for them to know. But they knew the Holy Spirit was coming on the Day of Pentecost, and that would happen in ten short days. Jesus had previously told them, "Behold I send the Promise of My Father upon you; but tarry in the city of Jerusalem until you endued with _____" (Luke 24:49). The disciples now had two reasons to stick close to Jerusalem. The gift of the Holy Spirit was coming, and also, Jesus would return to Jerusalem on His second coming. They didn't want to miss that! Read Zechariah 14:4 to find exactly where in Jerusalem Jesus will return at His Second Coming. _____

The Day of Pentecost (Promise of My Father) was a fulfillment of Old Testament prophecy. Joel 2:28a said "And it shall come to pass afterward that I will _____;" Jesus said in John 14:26 "But the Helper, the Holy Spirit, whom the Father will send in my name, He will _____."

Can you imagine a world without the Holy Spirit? How difficult would it be living without the presence of the Holy Spirit as it was done during the Old Testament times? _____
2 Thessalonians 2:7 said, "For the mystery of lawlessness is already at work; only He who now _____ will do so until He is taken out of the way." The Holy Spirit is holding back evil.

The disciples thought that the last week (seven years) of Daniel's prophecy (Tribulation) was to begin in the very near future, and then the kingdom (Millennium) would begin after The Tribulation. The first thing on the disciple's agenda was to replace Judas as the twelfth disciple. They needed one more disciple to rule over the twelve tribes during the Millennium age.

Soon after Jesus' ascension, Peter said in Acts 1:20b "Let another take [Judas's] office." There was a twofold requirement for the replacement disciple who replaced Judas (Acts 1:21-22). 1. _____2. _____

Matthias was elected. The twelfth disciple had been selected and disciples were ready for the kingdom.

Considering these requirements; could the Apostle Paul, (who is

148

at this time was persecuting Christians) have been considered for this position? _____

Peter and the disciples were prepared and ready to bring the nation of Israel to repentance. The Holy Spirit had been sent and Peter and John and the disciples began to boldly proclaim Jesus' name as their Messiah. Peter said to his brethren in Acts 3:19-21, "_____ (change of mind), therefore and be converted, that your sins may be blotted out, when the times of refreshing (Millennium) may come from the presence of the Lord, _____, who was was preached to you before, whom heaven must receive until the times of restoration of all things (curse is lifted), which God has spoken by the mouth of all His _____ since the world began."

Before the kingdom could come in, the entire nation of Israel (Acts 3:26) had to repent of not accepting and then killing their Messiah.

Acts 4:4 gave the progress for the total number of believers at that time was _____men. The momentum was growing. Annas and Caiaphas, the high priest, got into action. They thought they had gotten rid of this problem when they killed Jesus. In Acts 4:5-6, Annas and Caiaphas questioned the disciples and afterwards their action was (Acts 4:17)_____.

The expectations were very high as the believers waited for their Messiah to return and set up His kingdom. Here is an example of their anticipation. Acts 4:32-37 told of a Jewish group that sold and pooled their possessions together because they thought the Lord Jesus' return was imminent. Those Jewish believers combined resources to share together. Eventually the pool of money was used up after Israel failed as a nation to accept their Messiah. (Later during Paul's ministry, Paul asked believers to send money to this group in Jerusalem who were struggling financially. (Romans 15:26))

The Final Rejection of the Messiah

The momentum of the nation repenting was picking up speed. In Acts 6:7 said, "Then the word of God spread, and the number of the disciples multiplied greatly in Jerusalem, and a great many _____were obedient to the faith." It almost looked as if the nation of Israel was going to receive their Messiah. (It had been about three to seven years since the Resurrection.)

It all came to a crescendo on the day Stephen was brought before the Sanhedrin because of the accusation of blasphemy (Acts 6:8–15). What was said of Stephen? _____

In Acts 7, Stephen stood before the Sanhedrin and rehearsed the history of Israel. He began with Abraham and ended with Jesus. Stephen emphasized that Joseph's brothers did not recognize Joseph the first time they came to Egypt. Even the _____(Acts 7:13) time, the brothers returned to Egypt, they didn't recognize Joseph until he revealed himself to his brothers. The first time Moses offered to lead the Israelites out of Egypt, the people rejected him but left with Moses the _____time (Acts 7:25and 35-36). (Why did Stephen emphasize "the second time" for Moses and Joseph? Who else will come "the second time" that they persecuted and murdered? _____)

Stephen wound up his speech with this (Acts 7:51–53): "You stiff-necked and uncircumcised in heart and ears! You always resist the Holy Spirit; as your fathers did, so do you. Which of the prophets _____? And they killed those who foretold the coming of the Just One, of whom you now have become the betrayers and _____, who have received the law by the direction of angels and have _____."

The seventy-one members of the Sanhedrin were so angry at his speech that "they were _____and they gnashed at him with their teeth" (Acts 7:54). I don't know what it is like to gnash your teeth, but obviously, they were furious. Stephen told them the brutal truth. They didn't recognize their Messiah the first time Jesus showed Himself and they killed their Messiah.

Then to top it off, spirit-filled Stephen looked up and said in Acts 7:56, "Look! I see the _____ and the Son of Man standing at the right hand of God!" "Standing" is the keyword here.

The Sanhedrin knew their scripture. They were very familiar with Psalm 68:1, which said, "Let God _____, Let His enemies be scattered; Let those also who hate Him flee before Him," and Psalm 110:1, "The LORD said to my Lord, 'Sit at My right hand, till I make Your enemies Your footstool.'" Jesus was standing, ready to return. The Sanhedrin had refused their Messiah and they had been His enemy. "Then they cried out with a loud voice, _____ and ran at him with one accord" (Acts 7:57). That was the final straw. They stoned Stephen.

The nation of Israel's chance to receive their Messiah was lost—temporarily. But Israel will receive their Messiah the second time He returns.

Consider This

The Jews had to accept their Messiah as a nation to bring in the Tribulation or the 70th week and later the Millennium (Jesus ruling on earth). Stephen's appearance before the Sanhedrin would have been their best chance of that happening if the Sanhedrin had repented and recognized Jesus at that time. The Jewish people would probably have followed their lead, and repented, too.

Just as the entire nation came under the law (Exodus 19:8), they now had to repent and accept their Messiah as one nation. Peter said in Acts 3:26, "that every one of you" must repent and turn away from their iniquities of the rejection of their Messiah. One day that will happen. Zechariah 13:9b prophesied of that day when "Each one (Jewish nation) will say, _____."

Once the rejection was complete, a new character named _____ appeared on the scene. He was at the stoning of Stephen and was in agreement with Stephen's stoning. (Acts 7:58). But God was going to use him in a wonderful way. We'll pick up with Saul in lesson 7.

Take a moment to look at the first seven chapters of Acts to note if Gentiles were being included at this point. Do you see any reference to Gentiles? Check out these references that clearly indicate that so far, only the Jews were being addressed. (Acts 1:6, 2:5, 2:14, 2:22, 2:36, 2:38, 3:12, 3:25-26, 5:21, 5:31, 5:35)

I would recommend highlighting these passages in your Bible to aid in revealing only Jewish people were being offered the kingdom. But the Gentiles were going to be included in the near future.

Lesson 6 Review

On what day of the month of Nissan (April) was Jesus crucified?

_____

What annual Feast also took place on the same day as above? (Hint: the first one was in Egypt) _____

What were the qualifications of a sacrificial lamb?

_____

How many days was Jesus in the tomb? _____

Where was Jesus' Spirit during those days in the tomb? _____

Where is Hell/Hades? _____

Was anyone waiting for Jesus at the tomb on Resurrection Day?

_____

Jesus is the High Priest of the order of _____

What does "Begotten Son" mean? _____

What did the Feast of the Unleavened Bread on the 15th of Nissan illustrate what Jesus's death on the cross accomplished?

_____

What are the three parts of the harvest of the Feast of the First Fruits? _____

What event will cause the whole field of souls to be harvested?

_____

Notes

Notes

Lesson 7

"BEING JUSTIFIED FREELY BY HIS GRACE"

Read Romans through Titus (Gospel of Grace)

Overseas in the 1980s and 1990s we received very little news of the USA. The foreign newspapers carried their own internal news of that particular country but very little else. We received American newspapers from home by mail, but they often were late in arriving and dated. I called my parents, and my dad would bring me up to speed on some events. But for the most part, I felt isolated and uninformed.

It was a great day when international cable news entered our area. We kept that international channel turned on constantly for a solid month after its first day of broadcasting. Twenty-four-hour cable news opened our world. It felt like a fresh breeze as we joined the world again.

I think of Paul, who was handed the mantle after the Jews rejected their Messiah. He was given the Gospel of Grace, which opened up the world to the Gentiles. We Gentiles were now included. Gentiles began to understand who God is and the His great work of salvation, which God accomplished through His Son, Jesus. A fresh breeze of grace blew through the Gentile world.

Who Was Paul?

Saul used his Roman name, Paul, after his dramatic conversion on the road to Damascus rather than his Hebrew name, Saul. "Paul" meant "small or humble," and that was the manner Paul referred to himself in Ephesians 3:8 as "the _____ of all the saints" and in 1 Corinthians 15:9a "the _____ of the apostles." Jesus may have referred to Paul in Matthew 11:11b, when Jesus said, "But he who is least in the kingdom of heaven _____ than he" (John the Baptist). Could Jesus have meant Paul? What do you think? _____

In Philippians 3:5-6, Paul described himself.

- Hebrew/Jewish
- Tribe of Benjamin
- Pharisee (followed the law to the letter)
- Persecutor of the church
- Roman citizen- citizenship bestowed on his family probably by Emperor Pompey years earlier. (Acts 16:37–38; Acts 22:27-28)
- Highly educated (Acts 22:3—Paul said he was "educated at the feet of _____(top Rabbi at that time) according to the strict manner of the law of our fathers")

Paul was the man who wrote the thirteen books of the Gospel of Grace and changed the world with Christ being the foundation. The Jews went from **The Law** to the wonderful **Age of Grace**.
Who was the other educated man that God used in a tremendous way? _____

DAY 1

TRANSITIONS

We repatriated to the United States in 1998. It was an intense transition. We had spent over a decade overseas, and our culture here at home had changed a lot. We also weren't accustomed to living in a big city like Houston. When overseas, we visited our home of North Dakota on summer breaks. Our daughters had been accustomed to a lot of freedom to play and explore in our small childhood towns. Big city life was different.

Our sweet daughter, Brittani that year had just entered the second grade. She had never attended a school of eight hundred elementary-school children. Overseas they had been in small schools, filled with other international kids, and the girls had always been warmly received.

Brittani's elementary school encouraged parents to come and share lunch with their children. I jumped at the chance to see how Brittani was faring in school. She had a wonderful teacher, but I wondered about how many potential friends she had made. I arrived for lunch armed with a large pizza. I found Brittani in the lunchroom with her classmates, sitting on the end of the bench far from the rest of the crowd. I panicked. I set the pizza down and said, "Let's move near the other kids." Brittani politely refused. I lunched with Brittani off and on for a month, and always the same scenario, with Brittani sitting alone at the end of the bench. My mother's heart was breaking.

Arriving for lunch one day, I looked for Brittani and she wasn't in her usual spot at the end of the bench. I found her surrounded by her classmates. I spent very little one-on-one lunchtime with Brittani that day because of her chattering newfound friends. When Brittani came home from school later that afternoon, I asked her about the change. Brittani answered with a very matter of fact response. "I was waiting to see who I wanted to be my friend. If I chose too soon, I might have chosen the wrong ones." She understood the transition far better than I did.

Paul was going to make a transition. He changed companions and made a huge break from his usual Pharisee law-keeping group. In lesson 6, day 5, we left Paul/Saul holding the coats of the men who stoned Stephen in Acts 7. He was all for killing followers of Christ. But after the Road to Damascus experience in Acts 9, Paul was converted. Ananias in Acts 9 was afraid to meet up with Paul, who had the authority from the high priest to bind up the people who were followers of Christ. Paul was someone to be feared.

In Acts 9:15, the LORD said to Ananias, "For he (Paul) is a _____, to bear My name before _____ and kings and the children of Israel." After meeting him, Ananias found Paul's conversion was genuine.

Immediately after his conversion, Paul traveled from Damascus directly to Mount Sinai in Arabia. The same location where Moses received the law, Paul was going to receive the Gospel of Grace from the Lord Jesus.

Paul said in Galatians 1:15–18, "But when it pleased God, who separated me from my mother's womb and called me through His grace, to reveal His Son in me, that I might preach Him among the _____, I did not immediately confer with flesh and blood, nor did I go up to Jerusalem to those who _____, but I went into Arabia and returned again to Damascus. Then after _____ I went up to Jerusalem to see Peter, and remained with him fifteen days, But I saw _____ of the other apostles except James, the Lord's brother."

Why do you think Paul didn't go directly to Jerusalem and talk to the disciples after his conversion in Damascus? _____

Who gave the Gospel of Grace to Paul? Read the following verses for the answer. _____

Acts 20:24: "But none of these thing move me; nor do I count my life dear to myself, so that I may finish my race with joy, and the ministry which _____, to testify to the gospel of the grace of God."

Galatians 1:11–12: "But I make known to you, brethren, that the gospel which was preached by me is not according to man. For I neither received it from man, nor was I taught it, but it came _____."

1 Corinthians 9:1a: "Am I not an apostle? Am I not free? Have I _____ Jesus Christ our Lord?"

1 Corinthians 15:8: "Then last of all He (Jesus) _____ also, as by one born out of due time."

What is the *Gospel of Grace* that Paul was given by the Lord Jesus at Mt. Sinai? Paul spelled it out for us in 1 Corinthians 15:1-4. Paul said in verse two about the Gospel, "by which also you are _____". In verses 3-5 said, "For I delivered to you first of all that which I also received: that Christ _____for our sins according to the Scriptures, and that He _____, and that He _____ again the third day according to the Scriptures,"

Paul wasn't one of the original disciples of Jesus. He was bringing something completely new that Jesus revealed to him at Mount Sinai. First he will offer it to the Jews and then later to the Gentiles. It was going to be a hard journey. Even though the Gospel of Grace was a fresh breeze, many, especially the law keeping Jews found it hard to comprehend.

How did Paul compare to the other apostles? Read the following verses that Paul wrote defending his position.

o Second Corinthians 11:5: "For I consider that I am _____ to the most eminent apostles."

o Second Corinthians 11:23: "Are they ministers of Christ?--- I speak as a fool —_____ — in labors more abundant, in stripes beyond measure, in prisons more frequent, in deaths often."

o   Second Corinthians 12:11: "I have become a fool in boasting. You have compelled me, for I ought to have been commended by   you,   _____, though I am nothing."

Paul had a position that was criticized by many. He transitioned from persecutor of believers to proclaiming The Gospel of Grace. After reading the above scriptures, how did he compare to the disciples? _____

DAY 2

A DIVISION WAS MADE

In junior high, I had become friends with the more popular girls in my class. We met mornings in the library to chat. We always sat in the same places around the table until the bell rang for our first class of the day.

One weekend evening, one of my friend's older sisters offered to drive my new group and me around town. We jumped at the chance. We enjoyed the freedom of having a car rather than relying on bikes or parents to take us to the usual drive-ins or the bowling alley.

Later that evening, our driver suggested we leave town and go to a party down the road. It was a party with alcohol and packed with older students. It sounded so tempting. We could rub shoulders with the older crowd! Everyone was in for the adventure. As we got closer to leaving town, I started to feel nervous.

I spoke up, right before we exited town and said, "Could you take me home, please? My dad would kill me if he found out I attended the party."

The older sister promptly drove me to my home and dropped me off. Everyone called as I ran to my house, "See you on Monday."

The following Monday, I walked into the library, saw my usual place at the table, and sat down. As I sat down, my whole table of friends stood up in unison and exited the table, laughing uproariously. I sat alone in shock, letting it soak in, in those minutes before the bell rang for the start of school. I realized I had created a division. I didn't follow their rules. I was out of the group.

Paul created a division. He had been given The Gospel of Grace, but most of the Jews weren't ready to give up the law. The Jews had been steeped in the law and it's traditions for one thousand five hundred years, and now Paul was breaking from it. The law had been fulfilled, and sacrifices weren't necessary any more. But they loved the temple and all the traditions. The Book of Acts gives most of the events of this transitional time of leaving Law and understanding Grace.

Let's look at the sequence of events that created a *division* between law and grace and how the Age Of Grace was ushered in.

1. The First Event

Cornelius

Peter opened up the road to the Gentiles after the rejection of the Messiah by the Sanhedrin and Stephen's stoning. (Paul wasn't in the mix yet. He was at Mount Sinai, receiving the Gospel of Grace.) Peter had been given the keys to usher in the Gentiles (Matthew 16:19). Peter had a vision and saw a sheet lowered down three times of all the unclean beasts and the LORD told him could eat them all. Under the law they were all prohibited. How did Peter react to that vision? _____ (Acts 10:14).

Immediately after, Peter was sent by the Holy Spirit, and traveled to see Cornelius, a gentile. What did Peter say to Cornelius and his household in Acts 10:28? _____ Up until this point, Peter was a law-keeping Jew. He didn't eat with Gentiles and usually kept his distance.

While Peter spoke with Cornelius and preached Jesus the Messiah and salvation (Acts 10:34-42), Cornelius and his group believed and the Holy Spirit came upon the gentiles. This _____ Peter and the Jews with him in Acts 10:45. Peter and friends baptized the gentiles <u>after</u> their conversion.

What was astonishing? Not only had the Holy Spirit had been given to the Gentiles but also the sequence of salvation was reversed for the Gentiles. While the Jews had to repent, be baptized and <u>then</u> they received the Holy Spirit (Acts 2:38), the Gentiles immediately received the Holy Spirit after believing and baptism came later. What was the reason for that change? _____

Peter and the seven men returned to Jerusalem. When they came in contact with their fellow Jews, the Jews contended with Peter. Why did they contend with Peter in Acts 11:2–3? _____

The disciples preached the word right after the "Cornelius" event, but they were "preaching the word to no one but the _____" (Acts 11:19). Peter and the disciples were not going to the Gentiles. That was given to Paul to accomplish.

2. The Second Event

The Church at Antioch

The church in Jerusalem kept hearing about Gentile converts in Antioch. They didn't know what to do with these Gentile converts. They sent spirit-filled Barnabas to check it out. Barnabas recognized that Gentile converts were the beginning of something new. He realized it was "the _____ of God" (Acts 11:23) and he encouraged them. Barnabas went to seek _____ (Acts 11:25) rather than return to the church in Jerusalem. Barnabas and Paul joined up and began to minister together. The Gentiles were being included in the ministry.

Paul was the minister to the Gentiles and offered The Gospel of Grace. Peter was the minister to the Jews. Paul clarified in Galatians 2:7-9: "But on the contrary, then they saw that the gospel for the un-circumcised (Gentiles) had been _____, as the gospel to the circumcised (Jews) was to _____ (for He that worked effectively in Peter for the apostleship to the Circumcised, also worked effectively in me toward the Gentiles) and when James, Cephas (Peter) and John, who seemed to be pillars, perceived the grace that was given to me, they gave me and Barnabas the right hand of fellowship, that we should go to the _____ and they unto the circumcised."

The Gospel of Grace preached by Paul was hard to understand for Peter and the Jews. The temple was still up and running, and no one had told them to stop going to the temple and observing the Law. The Jews were waiting for Jesus to return again any day soon.

It was a confusing time of anticipation and wonder as the number of Gentile converts picked up speed. Peter said in Second Peter 3:15b-16, "as also our beloved brother Paul, according to the _____, has written to you, as also in all his epistles, speaking in them of these things, in which are _____, which untaught and unstable people twist to their own destruction, as they do also the rest of the Scriptures." Peter knew the Gospel of Grace, received by Paul was changing everything and it was hard to understand but Peter was in full agreement.

Do you think that it was hard to change the Jewish mindsets that Christ's sacrifice freed them from the law? _____

I had to change my mindset after living in Denver for eight years. We loved living in beautiful Denver. We took advantage of the mountains and hiking whenever we could. But suddenly, Mark found out he had been transferred to Houston. Our youngest daughter, Charissa, was a junior in high school, and we thought the logical scenario was for Charissa and me to remain in Denver until she graduated from high school. Mark would transfer alone until after her graduation.

Mark and I conferred together and decided that we would let Charissa make that decision to transfer immediately or wait to transfer after her graduation from high school, since it was mostly going to affect her. We presented both options and gave her time to consider them. We felt we knew which option she would choose.

A few nights later, she popped her head in the living room and told us she made her decision. She was ready to move to Houston! Our mouths dropped open. Mark was thrilled and made plans that evening to start moving our possessions to a storage unit in Houston. He was excited. I was shocked.

The next day, I took Charissa aside and reviewed all the disadvantages of the move. I was definitely trying to influence her decision and didn't think she had weighed her decision carefully. If Mark started hauling our excess furniture to Houston and we put our house on the market, it would be irreversible.

She stood firm in her decision.

We moved. The change to a new location started that night that Charissa told us her decision. We were soon on our way to Texas.

DAY 3

GENTILES AND THE LAW

While in China in 1986, the Chinese requested I teach some English classes. I didn't have any teaching materials with me, but they insisted because I was a teacher and spoke English with an admired American accent. I found myself in a chilly, unheated room, standing by an antique chalkboard, waiting as all my students were served steaming hot cups of tea. Most of the students were older respected men, uniformly dressed in their dull blue Mao suits and hats. They surprisingly had a fair amount of English under their belts. I was hamstringed by their reluctance to speak. None of them wanted to lose face and make a mistake in front of their peers. Because of that difficulty, I decided to teach them in a monologue-style format. I made up stories every day, and they would read along with me, which reduced their embarrassment. They would chuckle at the stories that depicted American life and some of its comical frustrations. Throughout the classes, I was impressed by their perseverance to learn about another culture and the English language. They were ready to make some changes.

The book of Acts is often called the "transitional book" because it spelled out the changes going from law to grace. Some made the changes and some fought the change. Paul and Barnabas began their ministry ministering with the Jews and were met with great opposition. In Acts 13:46, Paul said, "It was necessary that the word of God should be spoken to you _____; but since you reject it, and judge yourselves unworthy of everlasting life, behold, _____." Who heard the Gospel of Grace first? _____

Why did the Jews reject the Gospel of Grace in Acts 13:45-46?

_____

In Acts 13:50–51, the Jews kicked Paul and Barnabas out of Galatia. "But they (Paul and Barnabas) shook off the dust from their feet against them, and came to Iconium." (Shaking off the dust means to break completely with them.) Read Acts 14:19. What happened to Paul? _____

At the same time of the Jewish rejection, there was a lot of pressure applied to the Antioch Christian Church. The new Gentile converts were being told to make some changes. It was a tense time, as the law-keeping Jews insisted the Gentiles come under the burden of the law. The Jewish consensus was that the new Gentile converts were to be circumcised as Jews. Acts 15:1 says, "And certain men came down from Judea and taught the brethren, 'Unless you are _____ according to the custom of Moses, you _____.'"

The law-abiding men were sent from Jerusalem to Antioch to correct the situation. They didn't understand what God was doing. Paul and Barnabas had a big argument with these men from Jerusalem. It was decided that Paul and Barnabas and the men would go together to the council in Jerusalem to help decide if the Gentile converts needed to come under the law (Acts 15:2). When they arrived, Paul and Barnabas declared all the things God had done. (Read Romans 6:14b: "for you are not under _____ but under _____." This is a summation of what Paul revealed to them.)

Converted Pharisees in Acts 15:5 also rose up to insist that these new Gentile converts must follow the law. There was much disputing until Peter got into the mix. In Acts 15:7b, Peter stood up and said, "Men and brethren, you know how that a good while ago [twelve years ago, Peter made his trip to Cornelius] God chose among us, that by _____ should hear the word of the gospel, and believe."

In verse 9, Peter said, "There is no _____ between us and them." And in verse 10, Peter said, why put a yoke (the law) upon the necks of these believers, "which neither our fathers nor we were able to bear?"

After Peter spoke in verse 12, the audience quieted down and listened to Paul. Read verse 24. What decision was made? Law or no law?

_____

The Jewish council sent a letter with Paul to the Gentiles in Antioch. Acts 15:23–29 detailed what the Gentile converts, should do. Please write the council's instructions below.

_____

Paul received the Gospel of Grace and wanted the new Gentile converts to live in the wonderful freedom of grace. Grace had been paid for by Christ's sacrifice. Paul wanted the Gentiles to live as free men and not under the bondage of the law. What was the reaction of the Gentile converts when Paul and Barnabas gave them the letter from the council
(Acts 15:31)? _____

In chapters 16–28 of Acts, Paul ministered to both Jews and Gentiles. I can imagine Paul's sadness and frustration because he couldn't get through to the majority his own countrymen. Read what Paul said about his fellow Jews in Acts 28:27. Put it in your own words. _____

Paul made his final appeal to the Jews. Paul said in Acts 28:28, "Therefore let is be known to you that the salvation of God has been sent to the Gentiles, and they _____!" Paul turned to the Gentiles.

DAY 4

LAW WAS OVER AND THE AGE OF GRACE BEGAN

Paul, at the end of his twenty-five years of ministry, completed thirteen books of the Gospel of Grace, from the book of Romans to the book of Titus. The last book written was Second Timothy in 67 A.D. The completed Gospel of Grace was then circulated for three years before God allowed the Temple to be destroyed in 70 A.D. *Law was over.*

The Second Temple-Destroyed in 70 A.D.

Herod the Great, a great builder, began expanding the Second Temple in 19 B.C. and rebuilt it to a more magnificent scale by the time Jesus began His ministry. Herod the Great (Matthew 2:16–18) was also the same Herod that ordered the massacre of all children less than two years of age at the time of Jesus's birth.

Isn't God's timing precise? He didn't take the temple away until the Gospel of Grace was completed. One system replaced the other.

While visiting Israel in 2014, we toured the Western Wall in Jerusalem. It is the only section of wall that remains that encircled the Second Temple. We could see the pain on Jewish faces as they went to the wall to pray. They want their temple rebuilt so they can correctly follow the law.

The Jews have a Temple museum in Jerusalem that displays furniture, menorahs and the Levite priesthood robes in preparation for the future temple. They are ready for that third temple to be built so they can again begin sacrificing and observing the Law. (See the *Temple Institute* website for photos and information.) They have been without a temple for two thousand years. Many erroneously wait for their Messiah to come for the first time and don't realize He came right on time. They missed it.

Here are some verses of the Gospel of Grace that sum up this transition from law to grace. One is found in Ephesians 2:11-13: "Therefore remember that you, once Gentiles in the flesh---who are called Un-circumcision by what is called the Circumcision made in the flesh by hands—that at that time you were _____ being aliens from the common-wealth of Israel and _____, having no hope and without God in the world. But now _____ you who once were far off have been brought near by the _____ of Christ."

After reading the passage above, answer these questions.

> Are Gentiles included the covenants? _____
> Do Gentiles have hope? _____ What is the hope? _____
> What made the difference? _____
> Reading the verse below, how do we fulfill the law in the Age of Grace? _____

Romans 13:8: "Owe no one anything, except to love each other, for the one who loves another has fulfilled the law."

DAY 5

WAITING FOR MARRIAGE

"And to _____, whom He raised from the dead, even Jesus who _____ from the wrath to come." (1 Thessalonians 1:10)

Waiting for a special day is always hard to do, and yet the anticipation is a wonderful feeling. The week or two waiting to return to our family and friends in the United States after a year residing overseas was difficult at times. We wanted to go home, relax, and chat with our friends and family. I wanted to see those loving faces of our parents and siblings, just to take a rest.

When we would enter the United States and pass our passports to the customs officer, without fail, they passed them back with a warm smile and said, "Welcome home." That moment was so sweet because we knew we belonged and were citizens of this wonderful country. We were home.

Philippians 3:20 told us our citizenship is in heaven after we receive Christ as our Savior. This old earth is not our home. We are waiting to join our Bridegroom, Jesus. We wait to be at home with Jesus and feel that peace of being home.

Once we put our faith and trust in Jesus, our positions as believers are spelled out in the scripture. (There's much more in the scripture pertaining to our position in Christ; this is not a complete description.)

1. We are one in Christ as in a marriage (Galatians 3:28; Ephesians 4:4) Just as Adam and Eve were one flesh as a married couple; we are one with Christ because we are _____ to Him (Romans 7:4).
2. We are part of the _____ (1 Corinthians 12:12). Christ.
3. We will reign with Him one day during the Millennium. (2 Timothy 2:12).

This is so rich and incredible. It is hard to take in. What are your thoughts? _____

We wait, for Christ our Bridegroom to take us home, to live and know Him intimately for seven years. As His bride/church we will rule with Him on Earth during the Millennium. There is only one event of Daniel's prophecy left to take place before the final week and the Tribulation begins. It is when the antichrist signs a covenant for seven years with the nation of Israel. (Daniel 9:17) It is demonstrated in the second part of harvest of the field in The Feast of the First fruits (look back in *For Your Information* right after Christ's resurrection on day 15th of Nissan).

How do we know Jesus will take His Bride to heaven (the Rapture) before the Tribulation begins? Look at the following two points.

1. The church/body of Christ is told; we will not suffer the wrath of God (Revelation 6:16-17 and 15:7) that is poured out on the earth during the Tribulation. Read the following verses that told us the Bride of Christ (the Church or the Body of Christ) will not suffer wrath.
   Romans 1:18 _____
   Romans 5:9 _____
   Colossians 3:6 _____
   1 Thessalonians 5:9 _____
2. We know from the scriptures that law and grace cannot coexist together. (Only a short time was it allowed to

co-exist was when Apostle Paul was writing the Gospel of Grace.) Paul said in Romans 11:6: "And if by grace, then is it _____; otherwise grace is no longer grace. But if it is of works, _____: otherwise work is no longer work." The Third Temple will be up and operating during the seven years of the Tribulation and sacrificing will be resumed. The believers of the Age of Grace can no longer be on earth because we are saved through Grace. Paul said in Galatians 5:4: "you have become estranged from Christ, you who _____; you have fallen from grace." Those are strong words.

When the third temple is built and sacrifices are being offered again in the Tribulation, can Christ's Bride/Church, who was saved by grace, be present as the sacrifices are again being offered? _____ Jesus' work on the cross was complete and nothing can be added to it. No more sacrifices are needed and anything added would diminish Christ's sacrifice.

I wanted to leave a verse to ponder: Paul writes this verse with such tenderness for the Bride of Christ. Paul said in 2 Corinthians 11:2: "For I am jealous for you with godly jealousy, for I have _____ you to one husband that I may _____ to Christ." We are waiting for our Bridegroom. Just as Isaac met Rebekah in the field, we will meet Jesus in the air and He will take us home to heaven. A place He has prepared for us. At the end of the seven years (Tribulation), Jesus will return to the earth, just as He left, but this time on a white horse (Revelation Chapter 19). He will come to conquer and take the earth back from the stronghold of sin.

It is encouraging to know that we will be safely in heaven with our Bridegroom during the wrath of the Tribulation. Our hope is in the Lord, our Bridegroom, Jesus our Redeemer.

I pray that this study has given you the basic structure of the Bible and the message of hope, faith, and love. The Bible fits so perfectly together, and it is a beautiful plan of salvation and fulfillment of it all by our God, Lord, and Savior, Jesus Christ. I would encourage you to study Daniel and Revelation that reveal what will occur during the final seven years (Tribulation) or the seventieth week.

As the Body of Christ, the scriptures indicate we are not present at that time. The unsaved, will be here to endure this horrible seven years. We need to let them know of the coming events so they can come to know Jesus in a personal way before those final seven years commence.

Revelation 22:20: "Jesus said, 'Surely, I am coming quickly.'"

Review

Adam sinned and the earth was cursed. Who will take away the curse and has redeemed us? _____

How did the world fare in the years before the flood? _____

Why did God designate a people for His name? _____

What did God promise Abraham? _____

Why did God ask the Israelites to come under the Law?
_____

What other nations came under the law? _____

What is the Gospel of Grace? Jesus our God and Savior died, _____ **and** _____ **again.**

Did Israel as a nation recognize their Messiah? _____

When will Israel recognize their Messiah? _____

Who wrote the books of the Bible pertaining to Grace? _____

Are we under the Law any longer? _____

What needs to occur before the final week/seven years of the Tribulation will begin? _____

In Who do we need to put our faith and trust? _____

Notes

Notes

Notes